10 Steps to Dynamic Leadership

Practical models for immediate use!

The slim book with a wealth of ideas;
exciting, thought-provoking models for leadership!
—— John Kehoe, President
KBM Office Equipment

Jean Seville Suffield

10 Steps
to Dynamic Leadership

Practical models for immediate use!

Copyright ©2008 Jean Seville Suffield
Cover Graphic: Microsoft Clip Art
Electronic Makeup: Jane Dunant
Jean's Photo [Original]: Kim Hickey
Black & White Photo: Said Magdi
Advisor on Organization of Book: Kenneth L. Pierce
Editing: Lynn Sumida

Jean Seville Suffield, Author
10 Steps to Dynamic Leadership

1. 10 Steps (Leadership)
2. Applications of Choice Theory, Reality Therapy (Psychology)

ISBN   978-1-105-62115-4

PRINTED IN THE USA
Second Edition 2012

PRINTED IN CANADA
First Edition 2008
Imprimerie Marquis

©Choice-Makers
jeanseville@hotmail.com

Acknowledgements

Those who have helped me with this book, I salute and thank you. I am most grateful to Lynn Sumida and Ken Pierce for the learning I have gained from their insights. I offer special appreciation to Dr. William Glasser and Eric Jensen as my mentors.

Contents

Practical

Models

for

Immediate

Use!

Practical

Models

for

Immediate

Use!

Introduction

This valuable though slender book offers you essential steps in embracing leadership. It serves as a resource for quick-paced leaders or managers who want a guide to various concepts to see which they might explore further for their organization. If you are some one who has little time but would like a ready hands-on guide to help you reflect on what so many experts in various fields have to offer about leadership in today's market, then this book is for you.

Alice's Adventures in Wonderland and *Through the Looking-Glass* are the perfect catalysts for this AD-VENTURE into leadership because Alice's encounters reflect many challenges leaders face in the workplace: falling down the rabbit hole, encountering different types of people, working through several detours, taking many risks along the way and, of course, playing the great game of chess which offers a metaphor for life. Chess represents, for me, critical thinking within the organization. I enjoy Alice's self-reliance, self-confidence, openness and respect for those she encounters on an open plane of human action and interest, and her flexibility in adjusting to chaos around her. The realism within the fantasy world offers us the paradoxes and apparent contradictions which are the 'stuff' of human beings.

Have fun playing with the concepts!

Jean Seville Suffield

How to Use This Book

I offer you my perception of the 10 main steps to help you on the road in your journey to becoming the dynamic leader you want to be for your business, for your organization and for you, on a personal level, to grow in awareness and to gain new insights. The book may also serve as a guide for instructors with The William Glasser Institute and other Facilitators in the area of leadership to interlink ideas and generate critical thinking.

The steps are offered as part of the reflective process leaders undertake as they examine their thinking about what leadership means in the here and now. Reading the cited works paints a fuller picture of what the authors intended and broadens the knowledge, skill and further applications for leadership for those who want to make a difference within their organizations. Consider the steps as a map to which you may refer as often as required. It may become apparent you need to begin with the personal and collective visioning process to arrive at a sense of purpose for your organization. In contrast, this may prove unfruitful unless you and the people in your organization understand systems and systems thinking. As with any journey, beginning with 'yourself' best prepares you for the road ahead. As a leader, you may choose whichever step you perceive to be important or more relevant for you and your business.

I remember a saying from some years ago, "Now that I know all the answers, they changed the questions." Many years later comes the realization that there may not be any set answers but only those uncovered from within. There are only questions leading to the discovery of the interconnectedness of things!

10 Steps to Dynamic Leadership

'Would you tell me, please, which way I ought to go from here?"
"That depends a good deal on where you want to get to," said the Cat.
"I don't much care where –" said Alice. Then it doesn't matter which
"way you go," said the Cat.[2]

Alice's Adventures in Wonderland
Lewis Carroll (1832 – 1898)

Leaders need to find the path that is good for everyone in the organization. So, I invite you, as the leaders, to discover those concepts, innovations and practices, I want to entice you, to heighten your interest, and to challenge you to find an integrated wholeness for your organization. Alice serves as the catalyst on your journey and I believe that the HipBone Game, offered by Charles Cameron, forms the central image to help you and your organization develop and improve your critical thinking skills, essential to growth and productivity in any organization.

The HipBone activity explores concepts and insights in an atmosphere of cooperation and provides a useful tool for teaching creative thinking, conflict resolution and problem-solving in challenging, insightful, and thought-provoking ways. It may be easy or subtle - as you choose how to map your ideas onto the board positions. It helps to study basic human thought processes at the heart of creativity. Challenge yourself to provide the most interesting, curious, eccentric, elaborate, insightful and imaginative links you can make. It's not only "your turn" but more importantly, it's "your choice!"

The HipBone image is offered here at the beginning of the book for you to keep it in memory and to prime you for the steps to follow. It is also offered at the end of the book with specific instructions and some examples on its use. Remember, the answers are from within.

The WaterBird Board – HipBone Game³

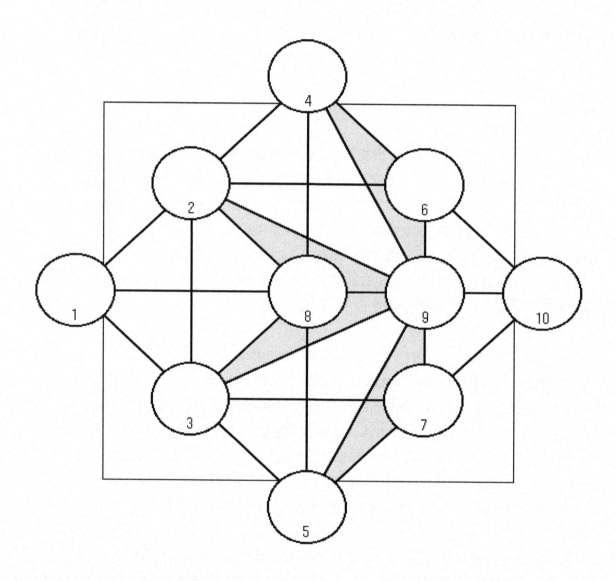

[Game and original Board by Charles Cameron, printed with permission. See endnote for entry.]

Step 1 Be Clear

Peter Senge's books, *The Fifth Discipline* and its companion, *The Fifth Discipline Fieldbook*, are seminal works about systems thinking and how it applies to organizations. I rely on *The Fifth Discipline Fieldbook* in this work and have acknowledged Senge's contributions as well as those of others, who have made innovative offerings to leadership. *The Fifth Discipline Fieldbook* has served me as an essential resource for my own learning and in training sessions over the years.

"Let's pretend . . . so that we can get through" [168], urges Alice, as she holds her kitten up to the looking-glass or mirror, which represents that wondrous affinity between man and imagination. Knowing who you are and reflecting on how you see yourself clarify what is important to you in your life. You then begin to understand the underlying values and beliefs you need to support the personal vision you are creating. It also assists you in determining where you want to go.

Be Clear about . . .

> ➢ how you see yourself
> ➢ what is important to you
> ➢ your personal living space

> ➢ the state of your health
> ➢ the relationships in your life
> ➢ your life's purpose

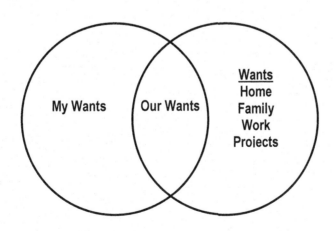

Personal Vision[4] – Creating the Life You Want to Live

Answer these questions for yourself, taking time to reflect on your answers, since they define who you are and the kind of person you want to be.

Imagine living your life the way you want to live it. What would your life look like? How would you describe what you have? What would you say inside your head, to yourself? What steps would you take to change your life in the direction you want to go?

> ➢ I really want . . .

> ➢ My life now looks like . . .

> ➢ The words that describe my life right now . . .

> ➢ My internal dialogue is . . .

> ➢ Changes I will make . . .

> ➢ I will take care of me by . . .

Personal Vision – Creating the Life You Want to Live

More areas[5] to explore . . .

> Self-image: If you could be exactly the kind of person you wanted to be, what qualities would you possess?

> Tangibles: List the material things that are important to you.

> Home: Describe your ideal home environment.

> Health: What do you want for health, fitness, athletics, or anything to do with your body?

> Relationships: What types of relationships are important for you to have with friends, family and others?

> Spirit: What do you want for your spirit / soul / life force / essence or being that sustains you in your life?

> Life Purpose: Imagine that your life has a unique purpose and that you can fulfill that purpose through your actions, through your relationships and by the way you live your life. Describe that purpose as another reflection of your aspirations. [6]

> Describe other areas in your life that are important to you.

Personal Vision – Creating the Life You Want to Live

Some definitions[7]

> Vision: From the Latin word 'videre' meaning 'to see.' The more detail you bring to the way you see where you want to go and how it will be when you get there, the more specific and clear your vision will be.

> Values: From the French word 'valoir' meaning 'to value' or 'hold worth.' Our values indicate the way we intend to operate or behave on a daily basis.

> Beliefs: From the Middle English 'bileven' meaning the mental acceptance of and conviction in the truth, actuality or validity of something. Accepted as true.

> Goals: Objectives that we commit to pursue within a set time.

> Mission: From the Latin word 'mittere' meaning 'to send.' The mission is the basic reason for the existence of the business organization. It is the act of declaring your collective purpose.

In discussing the meanings and origins of the above words, explore either with a partner or within the larger group the following statement:

Deep beliefs are often inconsistent
with espoused values in organizations.[8]

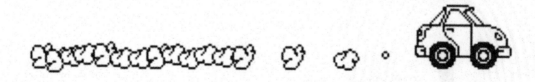

Personal Vision – Creating the Life You Want to Live

List the underlying values and beliefs needed to support your personal vision.

    <u>Vision</u>   <u>Values</u>   <u>Beliefs</u>

➢ Self-image:

➢ Tangibles:

➢ Home:

➢ Health:

➢ Relationships:

➢ Spirit:

➢ Life Purpose:

➢ How I Can Effect Change in my Life:

Personal Vision – Creating the Life You Want to Live

In the left hand column, list the key points you made in creating the life you say that you want for yourself [from page 5]. In the center column, describe what you perceive you have now. Check to see how close or how far away you are from your personal vision. Now write your action plan for creating and actualizing what you want for yourself in your personal life.

Ideal   What I have now   Action

Professional Vision[9] – Creating the Life You Want to Live

Reflecting on how you see yourself by building a professional vision clarifies what is important to you in your working life and helps you to begin to understand the underlying values and beliefs you need to support the professional vision you are creating.

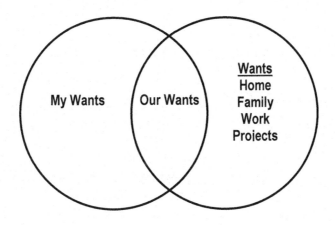

➢ I really want . . .

➢ My life now looks like . . .

➢ The words that describe my life right now . . .

➢ My internal dialogue is . . .

➢ Changes I will make . . .

Professional Vision – Creating the Life You Want to Live

More areas[10] to explore . . .

> Self-image: If you could be exactly the kind of person you wanted to be at work, what qualities would you possess?

> Tangibles: List the material things that are important to you at work.

> Work: Describe your ideal work environment.

> Health: What do you want for health, fitness, athletics, or anything to do with your body while you are working?

> Relationships: What types of relationships are important for you to have with others at work?

> Spirit: What do you want for your spirit / soul / life force / essence or being that sustains you in your working life?

> Life Purpose: Imagine that your working life has a unique purpose and that you can fulfill that purpose through your actions, through your relationships and by the way you live your life at work. Describe that purpose as another reflection of your aspirations.

> Describe other areas in your working life that are important to you.

Professional Vision – Creating the Life You Want to Live

List the underlying values and beliefs needed to support your professional vision.

<u>Vision</u>   <u>Values</u>   <u>Beliefs</u>

➢ Self-image:

➢ Tangibles:

➢ Work:

➢ Health:

➢ Relationships:

➢ Spirit:

➢ Life Purpose:

Professional Vision – Creating the Life You Want to Live

In the left hand column, list the key points you made in creating the life you say that you want for yourself at work [from page 10]. In the center column, describe what you perceive you have now. Check to see how close or how far away you are from your professional vision. Now write your action plan for creating and actualizing what you want for yourself in your professional or working life.

Ideal   What I have now   Action

Step 2 Build a Shared Vision

To support this creative process [shared visioning], people need to know that they have real freedom to say what they want about purpose, meaning and vision, with no limits, encumbrances, or reprisals. [Leaders] . . . must put aside their fear that "We must set the limits within which people can create vision, or they will run out of control." [11]

The Fifth Discipline Fieldbook
Peter Senge et al.

The croquet-ground in *Alice's* Adventures is chaotic: players not waiting to take turns; quarrelling and fighting; and the Queen furiously shouting "Off with his head!" or "Off with her head!" [98] as the only way the Queen had of settling difficulties.

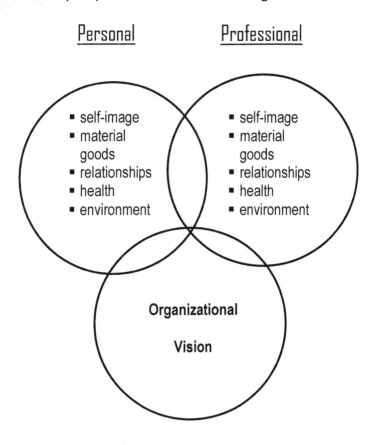

Building a Shared Vision – Creating the Organization You Want

The key to shared visioning lay in providing and ensuring an atmosphere of trust where people have the freedom to express themselves without reprisals. Leaders work on unifying any isolated parts of the organizational community. They know that fear and coercion diminish and destroy creativity so they are open to new ideas and allow the creative processes to evolve.

Pair & Share

Relate your story of how fear and coercion can destroy creativity in the workplace.

What behaviors do you use in the face of fear and/or coercion?

What changes did you make to nourish your creativity?

Did they work?

In retrospect, would you make the same choices again? Why or why not?

What behaviors do you use when your creativity is encouraged?

What type of climate brings out the best in you as a worker?

Are your values and beliefs in line with your organization?

What difference does it make when you share the vision co-created with the leaders in your organization?

Share with the larger group.

Building a Shared Vision – Creating the Organization You Want

More areas[12] to explore . . .

➢ Self-image: What kind of qualities do the people in the organization need in order to be self-sustaining?

➢ Tangibles: List the material things that the organization needs to do the job extraordinarily well within the organization.

➢ Work: Describe the ideal environment that nourishes the organization.

➢ Health: What does the organization want for the physical well-being of its staff?

➢ Relationships: What types of relationships are important for the organization?

➢ Spirit: What does the organization see as its driving spirit or essence as a sustaining force?

➢ Life Purpose: Together, through dialogue, consensus and team building, write a mission statement that reflects the unique purpose of the organization.

➢ How can you, through your actions, help fulfill the Mission of the organization?

➢ How can you, through your relationships, help fulfill the Mission of the organization?

➢ What is your understanding of the way the organization is to operate?

➢ Describe other areas that are important to you in the organization.

Building a Shared Vision – Creating the Organization You Want

List the underlying values and beliefs needed to support the organization.

Vision	Values	Beliefs

➢ Self-image:

➢ Tangibles:

➢ Work:

➢ Health:

➢ Relationships:

➢ Spirit:

➢ Life Purpose:

Building a Shared Vision – Creating the Organization You Want

In the left hand column, list the key points you made in creating the life you say that you want for the organization [from page 15]. In the center column, describe what you perceive you have now. Check to see how close or how far away you are from the organization's vision. Now write your action plan for creating and actualizing what kind of organization you want for yourself.

<u>Ideal</u>   <u>What I have now</u   <u>Action</u>

Building a Shared Vision – Clarifying Values[13]

> Values: From the French word 'valoir' meaning 'to value' or 'hold dear.'

Values are not hopes and dreams but things that identify the person or organization. Our values influence the way we intend or want to operate and are expressed through our behaviors on a daily basis.

Look through the following list and check those things that define you. This process helps the organization, which is made up of people, to define its values.

___ Accepting	___ Beautiful	___ Dashing
___ Accomplished	___ Befriending	___ Deliberate
___ Adept	___ Beguiling	___ Dependable
___ Adventurous	___ Capable	___ Devoted
___ Able to inspire others	___ Compassionate	___ Distinguished
___ Attractive	___ Daring	___ Dutiful

___ Enriching	___ Fantastic	___ Grand
___ Endearing	___ Forgiving	___ Graceful
___ Elegant	___ Free	___ Guiding
___ Endorsing	___ Fortunate	___ Happy
___ Energetic	___ Giving	___ Honest
___ Exhilarating	___ Glorious	___ Honourable

Building a Shared Vision — Clarifying Values

____ Harmonious

____ Helpful

____ Heroic

____ Imaginative

____ Innovative

____ Inspirational

____ Intuitive

____ Jovial

____ Just

____ Kind

____ Knowledgeable

____ Laudable

____ Learnéd

____ Loving

____ Magnificent

____ Masterful

____ Merciful

____ Model

____ Moral

____ Natural

____ Nourisher

____ Nurturer

____ Observer

____ Original

____ Passionate

____ Perceptive

____ Performing

____ Persistent

____ Placid

____ Playful

____ Prepared

____ Present

____ Questioning

____ Quick

____ Radiant

____ Rational

____ Reactionary

____ Refined

____ Responsive

____ Risk-taker

____ Savior

____ Server

____ Skeptical

____ Successful

____ Supportive

____ Synthesizer

____ Teacher

____ Tender

____ Thrilling

____ Truthful

____ Understanding

____ Unfailing

____ Uplifting

____ Venturous

Reflect on the items above.

Choose <u>nine</u> [9] that define you.

Place these values in three groups of three:
the top three, middle three and bottom three.

Building a Shared Vision – Clarifying Values

Values List:

Column 1	Column 2	Column 3
1. Passionate	4. Performing	7. Supportive
2. Connected	5. Playful	8. Compassionate
3. Creative	6. Inspirational	9. Aware

Complete the following two sentences using any three adjectives you can imagine.

First sentence: When I am at my very best, I am (insert three adjectives).
Example: When I am at my very best, I am *relaxed, trusting* and *open*.

Second sentence: When I am at my very worst, I am (insert three adjectives.)
Example: When I am at my very worst, I am *fearful, distrusting* and *sad*.

Try three (3) more examples using fictitious people (E.g. characters from a novel, political figures)

When I am at my very best, I am _____ _____ and _____ .
When I am at my very worst, I am _____ _____ and _____ .

When I am at my very best, I am _____ _____ and _____ .
When I am at my very worst, I am _____ _____ and _____ .

When I am at my very best, I am _____ _____ and _____ .
When I am at my very worst, I am _____ _____ and _____ .

Building a Shared Vision – Discovering Your Individual Mission

➢ Mission: From the Latin word 'mittere' meaning 'to send.' The mission is the basic reason for the existence of the business organization. It is the act of declaring your collective purpose.

Discovering your mission as an individual enables the whole team to understand one another and assists the organization in writing its Mission Statement.

The following questions may prove helpful in discovering your mission.[14]

- ○ What would you be doing if money were not a concern?

- ○ What would you be doing if education were not a concern?

- ○ What would you be doing if appearance were not a concern?

- ○ What would you be doing if success were assured?

- ○ What do you really love doing?

Write a Mission Statement for each of the nine values you selected on page 19.

1. Choose one of your nine values.

2. Think about what you want to do about that value, how you want to use it, and what you wish to accomplish with it.

3. Write it down. [See the following page for examples].

4. Repeat this process eight more times.

Building a Shared Vision – Discovering Your Individual Mission

Some examples using my values list from the top of page 20.

My mission is to <u>inspire</u> others through excellence in teaching to assist them in exploring and setting their life goals.

My mission is to be <u>passionate</u> about what I believe through teaching specific options to others in assisting them to evaluate their life choices.

My mission is to be <u>connected</u> to others through inspirational teaching and attentive listening while assisting them in building healthy relationships.

Now write your <u>nine</u> mission statements from the list of values that you generated for yourself.

> ➤

> ➤

> ➤

> ➤

> ➤

> ➤

> ➤

> ➤

> ➤

Co-creating a Shared Vision – The Mission of the Organization

Team Activity[15]

The group members form teams to facilitate brainstorming and discussion of questions outlined on page 24 in order to review strengths and to offer methods of evaluating behaviors.

Team Name   Strengths   Team Logo

Team Cheer

Wants   Values/Beliefs

Actions

Ways to Measure Success

Mission Statement for the Team

Co-creating a Shared Vision – The Mission of the Organization

Part I Envisioning the Future

Each team shares perceptions[16] of the following questions to express the identity of each team member, what each member wants for the organization, how the team will get there and how team members can measure the effectiveness of their choices.

What do we want for ourselves in the organization?

What kind of person do we want to be in the organization?

Who are the stakeholders?

In what ways are the stakeholders important to us?

What do we have that is of value to the stakeholders?

In what ways do we value our product(s)?

How can we maintain that value for the next five-year period?

What do we see as our purpose?

Describe this purpose in all its detail.

How can we compete in the marketplace?

What impact do we and our product have in the marketplace?

What are our values and beliefs that sustain us as an organization?

What are our behaviors when things are going well?

What process do we have in place when things aren't going so well?

How will we measure our success?

Co-creating a Shared Vision – The Mission of the Organization

Following the same process for brainstorming and dialogue on page 24, the teams now review what is presently happening within the organization.

<u>Part II Current Reality</u>

What is currently happening in our organization?

What do staff members want?

What are indicators that we are presently meeting the goals of quality we have set for ourselves?

How are we measuring our success in regard to:

> How we see ourselves

> What tangible things are important to us

> The daily work environment, such as business travel and stress

> Our health to work at our optimal best, periods of relaxation

> Our relationships within the organization

> The spirit or life force that connects us

Co-creating a Shared Vision – The Mission of the Organization

All [of us] are caught in an inescapable network of mutuality, tied in a single garment of destiny. Whatever affects one directly, affects all indirectly.[17]

Martin Luther King, Jr.
Nobel Peace Prize 1964
Civil Rights Leader (1929 - 1968)

Part III Co-verification of Values & Beliefs

Teams look at their future visioning [page 24] in light of the current reality [page 25] and examine their perceptions in relation to their values and beliefs.

Teams now share their future visioning with the larger group, their current reality and their values and beliefs.

Future   Current   Values/Beliefs

Teams share their mission statements and arrive at one that all members of the group can accept.

Step 3 Surrender Control

The only person you can
control is yourself! [18]
Choice Theory:
A New Psychology of Personal Freedom
William Glasser, M. D.

No matter how hard Alice tries, she cannot control the croquet-ground: " . . . the croquet balls are live hedgehogs, the mallets live flamingos and the soldiers, doubled up on hands and feet upside down, form the arches" [100]. Alice can only control herself, a crucial tenet of Choice Theory® that explains human behavior.

Choice Theory® forms the basis of all that Dr. Glasser now teaches. His main focus is on mental health and the delivery of the health care system mainly in the United States. His ideas about mental health and about building and maintaining healthy relationships, reflected in his recent book *Eight Steps to a Happier Marriage,* apply to leadership as well. As long as there are fear and coercion within any relationship or within a business or organization, that relationship is doomed to failure. [19]

The word 'surrender' [20] is taken from Peter Senge in *Presence* when he and the other authors speak of "surrendering control' that evolves into "surrending into commitment." This act of 'surrending' provides the gateway for leaders to operate from their deepest purpose within the big picture of the larger whole.

Triangle [21] - Needs Underlying Quality World Pictures

In small groups of five (5), have team members brainstorm what they want for themselves at work in order to understand the role that needs and perceptions play in behaviors. Dr. Glasser explains that we do not satisfy our needs directly but through the pictures we have in our 'Quality World." The Quality World is a way of describing the pictures we have in our heads, of the way we want things to be.

Surrendering Control - Understanding the Role of Perception

Team members write as many ideas as they can think about, writing one item per sticky note. Once they have done this, the facilitator works through a sample so team members understand what is meant by Quality World and needs. Plot these on a triangle explaining that, with each one, the group is satisfying one or more of their basic needs, and matching a picture or pictures in their Quality World.

trusting one another   fun working together   material resources
knowing the plan   flexible hours   ability to make choices

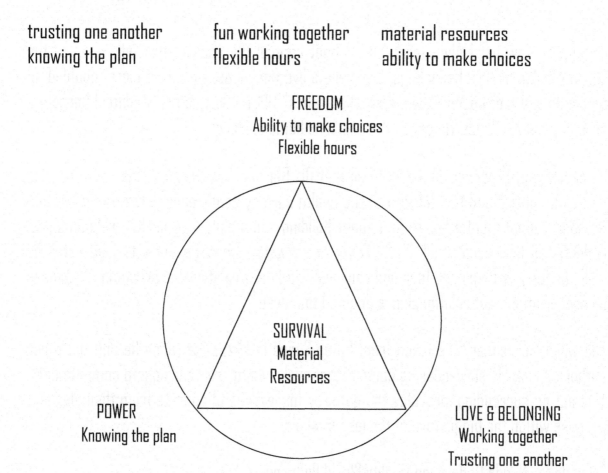

FREEDOM
Ability to make choices
Flexible hours

SURVIVAL
Material
Resources

POWER
Knowing the plan

LOVE & BELONGING
Working together
Trusting one another

Members will have different opinions about where to place the items and this is in keeping with individual perceptions. Encourage a discussion about the pictures in their Quality World as it relates to what they really want for themselves at work. Encourage them to provide as much detail as possible.

Surrendering Control - Understanding the Role of Perception

> When people try to force us to do things we do not want to do, because we do not find it need-satisfying because it does not honor what we value, we feel as if we have lost control of ourselves.[22]
>
> Using Lead Management on Purpose
> Kenneth L. Pierce

The Illusion of Controlling Others

Working in team groups of five (5), brainstorm the types of behaviors we use on others to get them to do what we want and the behaviors that others use on us to get us to do what they want us to do! Again, use one behavior per sticky note so all behaviors may be posted on flip chart paper.

Have members place the coercive behaviors on the left side of the flip chart paper and the supportive or caring behaviors on the right side. Most often the caring behaviors, which Dr. Glasser calls "Choice Theory Habits," are fewer in number. What members might observe is that the controlling, coercive behaviors or the "Deadly Habits" often prevail. If we regroup these behaviors, we may find them in the shorter list suggested by Dr. Glasser.

7 Deadly Habits
That Destroy Relationships

7 Choice Theory® Habits
That Strengthen Relationships

7 Deadly Habits	7 Choice Theory® Habits
Complaining	Accepting
Blaming	Befriending
Criticizing	Encouraging
Nagging	Listening
Punishing	Negotiating
Threatening	Supporting
Rewarding to Control Others	Trusting

Surrendering Control - Understanding the Role of Perception

We know we often use the behaviors that weaken and maybe even sever relationships. The goal is to help each other learn to use the Choice Theory® Habits more and more often so that the relationships are strengthened.

External Controlling Behaviors

➡ guilt and humiliation

➡ negative reinforcement

- physical
- anger – verbal
- intimidation
- threats
- punishment

➡ friendship (using a relationship to manipulate)

➡ bribery (rewarding to control others)

➡ monitor (looking at consequences)

Lead

to

Conformity,

Coercion

&

Fear

Internal Controlling Behaviors

➡ friendships (building & maintaining friendships – not manipulative)

➡ awareness of own behaviors

➡ focus on responsibility

➡ self-evaluation

Build

&

Nourish

Healthy

Relationships

Surrendering Control - Understanding the Role of Perception

Who can you control?

<u>The Knot on the Dot</u>[23]

Materials: -   Large rubber bands in various colors - two per team
              -    A notepad with a large circle drawn on one sheet of paper

Configuration: Team members form pairs with Person A and Person B seated, facing one another with the notepad balanced on their knees. The two rubber bands are interlocked prior to the activity.

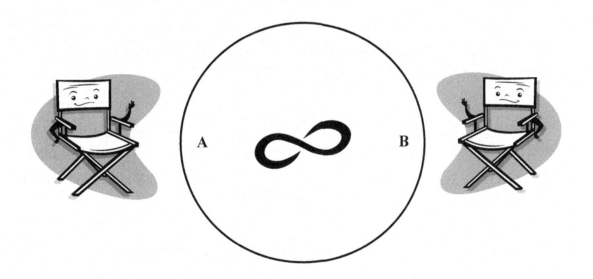

Working in pairs with interlocking rubber bands, Person A and Person B assume the roles of Manager and Employee. They work through the scenario given on the following page, presenting each other's point of view in a "push/pull" motion, and always attempting to maintain the position of their knot on their dot, thus experiencing kinesthetically the concept of control.

Surrendering Control - Understanding the Role of Perception

Scenario: John, who is a team leader, has been working for the company for two months and has been arriving late mainly for meetings. As the department manager, you have arranged a time to meet with him and discuss the situation.

1. Role-play this scenario with Person A playing the role of John, the employee and Person B playing the role of the manager. You have two (2) minutes to interrelate with your employee in a traditional way with external controlling behaviors. Then, reverse roles with Person A playing the role of the manager and Person B playing the role of John, the employee, again using controlling behaviors to get your point of view across.

2. With your partner, brainstorm the types of behaviors you each used in trying to relate to John in a traditional manner.

3. Now, replay the scenario in a creative way that demonstrates that you wish to focus on the quality of the relationship; therefore, using behaviors to get your point of view across in such a way that you maintain or perhaps even improve the relationship you have with John, thus moving closer rather than further away.

4. Now, brainstorm with your partner the different behaviors you used and their effectiveness compared to the external controlling behaviors used earlier.

5. Debrief in the larger group.
   - What behaviors did you use in trying to control the other person?

   - What shift occurred in the second role-play?

   - What did you notice about the rubber bands?

Surrendering Control - Understanding the Role of Perception

Value of The Knot on the Dot Activity

Some of the reasons for using The Knot on the Dot Activity are outlined below. What value do you perceive in this activity? What are other ways of using this activity or others similar to it to help understand control issues and leadership?

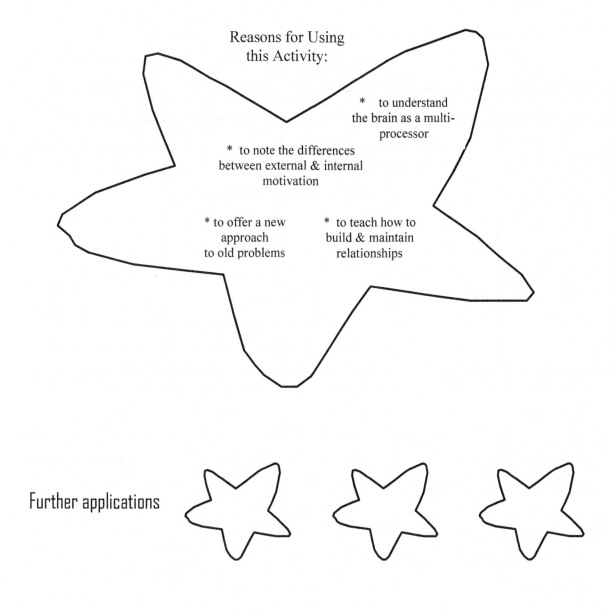

Reasons for Using this Activity:

* to understand the brain as a multi-processor

* to note the differences between external & internal motivation

* to offer a new approach to old problems

* to teach how to build & maintain relationships

Further applications

Surrendering Control - Understanding the Role of Perception

Pete's Pathogram[24]

1st column: What I want or my perception of the strength of my need.

2nd column: My perception of what I have or degree of satisfaction I enjoy.

3rd column: The effort I make to satisfy this need. Is it working? Do I need or want to change my picture of what I say I want?

Plan: Do I need a new plan? A more effective plan? How can I improve?

Personal Life

Finance / Safety	Love & Friendship	Power / Success	Freedom / Choices	Fun

A. Peterson & G. Parr. *Pathogram: A Visual Aid to Obtain Focus and Commitment* (Journal of Reality Therapy, Fall, 1982: 18-22)

<u>Debrief through Pair Discussion</u>: Notice on a scale of 1 to 10, by filling in the columns, what you want for yourself in your personal life under Finance and Safety, which is the Survival Need expressed differently. Repeat the exercise for the other four needs.

What is your perception of what you have? How hard are you working for it? Are you satisfied? What changes might you make? Be specific.

Surrendering Control - Understanding the Role of Perception

Pete's Pathogram

1st column: What I want or my perception of the strength of my need.

2nd column: My perception of what I have or degree of satisfaction I enjoy.

3rd column: The effort I make to satisfy this need. Is it working? Do I need or want to change my picture of what I say I want?

Plan: Do I need a new plan? A more effective plan? How can I improve?

Professional Life

Finance / Safety			Love & Friendship			Power / Success			Freedom / Choices			Fun		

A. Peterson & G. Parr. *Pathogram: A Visual Aid to Obtain Focus and Commitment* (Journal of Reality Therapy, Fall, 1982: 18-22)

Notice what you want for yourself in your professional life under Finance and Safety. Repeat the exercise for the other four needs.

What is your perception of what you have? How hard are you working for it? Are you satisfied? What changes might you make? Be specific. What influence do you have?

Step 4 Build Learning Networks

> You are mentally healthy if you enjoy being with most of the people you know, especially with the important people in your life . . . You are creative in what you attempt and may enjoy more of your potential than you ever thought possible. - you will see that the focus [of mental health] is on relationships.[26]
>
> Defining Mental Health as a
> Mental Health Issue
> William Glasser, M.D.

When the kitten tangles the wool in *Through the Looking-Glass,* Alice catches her and says, "Oh, you wicked, wicked little thing!" [164] giving it a little kiss to make it understand that it is in disgrace. This relationship is 'curious and curiouser' and the relationship remains intact. Let us now examine our personal relationships.

Quality Relationships with Family and Friends

1. Describe what a 'Quality' relationship, with either members of your family or friends, means to you.

    Family   Friends

2. Which family members and friends have a special relationship with you? Why?

3. What behaviors do you use to maintain this Quality relationship with family and friends?

    Family   Friends

4. Describe the process you have in place to resolve conflicts that may arise with family and friends.

Building Learning Networks - Relationships

To link all of these multiple communities together, the organization depends on its informal networks – communication channels where people talk easily and freely . . . As members of a community, we need to meet in person when we talk about what we really care about.[25]

The Fifth Discipline Fieldbook

Peter Senge et al.

Quality Relationships within the Organization

1.   Describe what 'Quality' relationships mean to you at work.

2.   Who do you consider your friends within the organization?

3.   In what ways are you closer to some colleagues than others?

4.   What behaviors do you use to maintain your friendships at work?

5.   What processes do you have in place to resolve conflicts at work?

6.   To what degree do these processes work?

7.   What strengths do you bring to your family and friends?

8.   What strengths do you bring to the organization?

9.   Under what conditions do you do your best work?

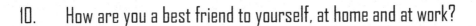

10.   How are you a best friend to yourself, at home and at work?

Building Learning Networks - Relationships

> Lead Managers find that as long as they take a friendly interest in what the workers are doing, asking them only to do useful work and to evaluate what they do, workers will not take advantage of their relationship. They will work much harder than if the manager is aloof or unfriendly.[27]
>
> Using Lead Management on Purpose
> Kenneth L. Pierce

In *Using Lead Management on Purpose*, Pierce offers seven key points on how empowered relationships create quality. Reframing the statements into questions facilitates a dialogue for leaders and team members.

Seven Key Points[28]

Define your understanding of quality relationships in the workplace. Then in pairs or as teams, dialogue on the following:

1. How do quality relationships produce consistent quality products?

2. In what ways does it help workers when leaders share who they are and what they stand for?

3. How does 'walking the talk' by leaders foster a sense of responsibility in the workers?

4. How are the roles of leaders different from those of their employees?

5. What impact do leaders have when they avoid the seven deadly behaviors that impede growth in the workplace?

6. What impact do leaders have when they exhibit the Choice Theory® behaviors in the workplace?

Building Learning Networks - Relationships

> We humans also deal better with stressors when we have outlets for frustration – punch a wall, take a run, find solace in a hobby. [There is an additional way . . .] Social support networks – it helps to have a shoulder to cry on, a hand to hold, an ear to listen to you, someone to cradle you and to tell you it will be okay.[29]
>
> Why Zebras Don't Get Ulcers
Robert M. Sapolsky

1. <u>Listen carefully in a sincere manner.</u>[30] Don't trivialize the issue or situation. If it's important to the other person, then consider it IMPORTANT.

Many perceive that we have lost the art of listening. How many times do you find yourself speaking with someone and they are doing something else: clearing their desk, checking their agenda items, making a notation, filing some paper?

List some listening skills important to the listening process.

➢

➢

2. <u>Seek to understand</u>. In this sense, you are in the other person's shoes, as it were, looking at the situation or issue from his or her point of view or perception.

Asking questions often helps to increase our knowledge, and to develop a clearer understanding of the situation. New information helps us to see situations differently and change our perceptions.

Pair and share a personal story that helped you change your perception of a person or situation. What conclusions did you draw from the experience?

Building Learning Networks - Relationships

3. <u>Present your point of view</u> or perception in a calm way only if both of you are in a listening mode. If not, set a time [within the next hour] to discuss the issue calmly.

Giving people time to get to know one another better, through shared visioning and community networking, helps diminish anger and aggression.

Many companies understand the time-pressured challenges their staff members face and offer Fitness Club memberships to their employees.

Pair and share other ways to help people manage their stressors at work.

➢

➢

4. <u>Re-evaluate your own needs</u> using Pete's Pathogram to see which need(s) is not being satisfied.

5. <u>Re-examine your own behaviors</u> in terms of using external or internal controlling behaviors with the other person.

6. <u>Evaluate</u> how you would want to deal with the same situation in the future.

7. <u>Remember that the relationship is the key.</u> Ask yourself, "Is this [action] going to bring me closer to the other person or move me further away?

How do leaders handle: a) the bottom line   b) the disgruntled employee
c) the necessity of firing a staff member   d) poor performance

Building Learning Networks - Relationships & Decision-Making

8. <u>Help others develop a sense of responsibility</u>[31] to make more effective decisions.

> Believe that "People are Responsible for What Happens to them."
>> - give them lots of practice
>> - let them face their responsibilities
>> - be non-judgmental
>> - allow for natural consequences

> The more they are responsible for their behavior, the better they'll be at accepting responsibility.

> Help them be aware of all the times that they are deciding what to do.

> Outline alternatives making sure everyone can live with them.

> Make sure you know the differences between punishments and consequences.

> Follow through on what the person chooses.

> Be consistent and clear.

> Let them face their responsibilities.

> Discuss a vision for the future but, above all, maintain a supportive work environment!

Pair and Share any two of the above statements and give examples from your experience.

Building Learning Networks - Relationships & Truth[32]

Telling the truth, not the 'absolute truth' but the truth as a person sees it, brings conflict between honesty and loyalty in many organizations. Peter Senge explains that longstanding attitudes, rewards and incentives are so deeply engrained within organizations that they come first before loyalty to the truth. To deny the truth is to deny one's own perceptions. The following questions may prove helpful in understanding organizational culture and what is openly stated but not practiced or what is hidden but nevertheless accepted practice.

1. Describe an instance within your company when your truthfulness was not acknowledged as helpful to the organization.

2. How did you express the truth? What was your intent?

3. Share with a partner, from your own experiences, the formal and informal punishments for speaking out. Share with the larger group.

4. What context and training can organizations provide for the truth?

5. How can leaders remain loyal to the spirit of the truth if they cannot divulge personal information? For example:

   ➤ staff member does not get the promotion others expect

   ➤ staff member was declared 'redundant' or 'surplus'

What type of policy or policies help to create a safe haven for telling the truth within an organization?

Step 5 Be Open To Mental Models

"Dear, dear! How queer everything is today! and yesterday things went on just as usual" [22]. Just as Alice reflects upon her experiences and continually tries to clarify what she is perceiving, leaders, who are open to other ways of seeing the world, improve their internal pictures and see how these shape their actions and decisions. Here are some mental models for reflection.

Dr. William Glasser's Choice Theory® is the basis for all the programs taught by The William Glasser Institute.[33] It states that all we do is behave, that almost all behavior is chosen, and that we are driven by our genes to satisfy five basic needs. Dr. Glasser uses the car analogy to indicate that what "drives" the car is the picture a person has of the way he wants things to be and s/he makes choices in order to match that picture and satisfy one or more of the basic needs for survival, love & belonging, power, freedom and fun. All behavior is total with four components operating concurrently: acting, thinking, feeling and physiology. Almost all people can relate to the car analogy and can understand that it is through acting and thinking that one can effect a change in feeling and physiology. *Choice Theory: A New Psychology of Personal Freedom* is the primary text for all that is taught by the Institute. A detailed explanation on Total Behavior may be found on page 66.

Reality Therapy is a method of counseling that Dr. Glasser has been teaching since 1965. It is the art of creating a meaningful relationship, and through that relationship, helping clients make more effective choices in their lives. It is the process of counseling based on Choice Theory®. Reality Therapy is the application of Choice Theory® and its success is dependent on the counselor's familiarity with and knowledge of Choice Theory®.

Mental Models - Leadership in Action

Leadership[34]

The following activity highlights the interrelationship between Reality Therapy and Choice Theory® and encourages teams to list their perceptions about how they see leadership, boss management and laissez-faire management along a continuum.

Reality Therapy	Boss	Leader	Laissez-faire	Choice Theory®
Climate - Environment				Needs - Satisfaction
Wants In Detail				Quality World Pictures
Present Behaviors				Total Behaviors
Self-Evaluation				Comparing Place
Plan				Behavioral System
Level of Commitment				Plan into New Action

Questions to facilitate the group process

1. What is the type of climate you would find in a boss-managed organization?
2. How do most employees satisfy their needs in a boss-managed place?
3. What 'wants' are usually expressed by the staff in a boss-led system?
4. Describe the Quality World of individuals in a boss-led system.
5. What are the workers or employees doing in a boss-led organization?

[Look at the total behavior of the boss and staff].

Mental Models - Leadership in Action

6.   Discuss the four components of total behavior [acting, thinking, feeling, physiology] for at least two of the behaviors one would observe in a boss-led environment.

7.   Who does the evaluating in a boss-led system?

8.   Describe the types of plans you might hear in a boss-led workplace.

9.   What type of commitment do you find in boss-led establishments?

10.   How are plans put into place?

In a similar manner, encourage teams to complete the grid on page 44.

Have teams report on their perceptions of the boss-managed workplace, the laissez-faire establishment and one that encourages and promotes leadership.

Levels of Commitment to Change[35] – Discuss in pairs and share with the larger group.

1. Denial   I don't even admit that the problem exists.

2. Awareness   I don't want to do anything about it.

3. Empty Wanting   I want the outcome but I don't want to make plans.

4. Trying   I'll try.

5. Best Effort   I will do my best.

6. Total Commitment   I'll do whatever it takes!

Mental Models - Leadership in Action

Miruspoint® Facilitators Inc. is a company dedicated to helping people evolve out of fear and into joy, peace and well-being. Lynn Sumida, co-founder and owner of Miruspoint, offers this perspective:

> *Our capacity to live from our heart and not just our brain, is the evolutionary jump that we need to make as human beings. This shift is so fundamental, it is like we change our identity, from one based on all the things we do, to an identity that truly reflects our essence.*[36]

Whether we are leading as a manager, a parent or a volunteer, the ability to be a really effective leader often rests, not on skill, but on a leader's ability to be fully present and open in their attitude and approach to others. At a cellular level, biology has shown our cells are either in "protection" or "growth" mode. In other words, we are either "open or closed." It doesn't matter what our words say, if underneath we feel afraid, angry or hurt. When we feel the need to protect ourselves, we are unable to really be open to others or the possibilities that exist.

Prime Potential®, developed by Miruspoint®, is a profound process that allows individuals to zero in on what is specifically blocking their ability to be open and have the confidence, joy, peace and balance in their lives. Miruspoint discovered in their work with people, that fear is often tied to the basic needs that Dr. Glasser described. We fear being rejected or alone, being devalued or powerless, restricted or controlled. If we feel emotionally unsafe, it translates in the body, as if we are unsafe physically. This fear can be rampant in our system or lie dormant, like a virus and only show up in certain circumstances. When this fear is addressed in the nervous system, people experience profound changes at a core level, more rapidly than they had thought possible. The challenge today, for leaders in our fast-paced, demanding world, is to lead from a place of openness and heart.

Mental Models - Leadership in Action

One activity that stands out for many people who have experienced Prime Potential ™ is doing the Life Satisfaction Index. The starting point in any change process is to know where you are starting from. This usually requires frankly assessing where you are currently. Instinctively we resist this because we sense it will be painful and yet ultimately it is freeing. Below is the first part of the Life Satisfaction Index. Filling it out will not change your life per se, but it will activate within you the desire for change. [Printed with permission.]

Life Satisfaction Index[37]

Shade the portion of the circle that represents how much of your life is currently **exactly** the way you would like it to be. Be as honest as you can, because as the saying goes "The truth will set you free." This information will assist you in your reflections on the question, "What's stopping you?"

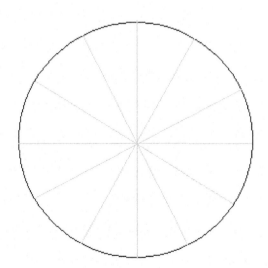

My life as I now perceive it to be.   Date: _____

Mental Models - Leadership in Action

Perceptual Change[38] is about expanding and articulating our deeply held beliefs about learning and working.

Seeing how new strategies and
approaches naturally emerge
out of a shift in our assumptions.

New Mental Models

Espoused beliefs = statements and actions that
reflect what we would like
to be true or think others
expect to hear or see.

> We often subsume new approaches to old beliefs. There is often a gap or mismatch between what we say we believe and what we do.
>
> Give some examples from your experience of this statement.

Mental Models - Leadership in Action

Kenneth L. Pierce is a facilitator of *The Demartini Method*® offered through weekend workshops entitled "The Breakthrough Experience." *The Demartini Method*® [*The Quantum Collapse Process*®] is a breakthrough self-discovery process that helps individuals transform any type of conflict or stress into varying states of love and gratefulness to achieve greater balance in seven areas of one's life. Understanding the physical universe and knowing how it operates assist individuals in aligning one's life with a personal sense of purpose. This life purpose becomes the spiritual guide for transformational change.

Here is one activity which exemplifies the depth of training "The Breakthrough Experience" offers. If I look at the <u>Mental</u> sphere of my life,[40] listening to my heart as a guide, being the master of my own destiny, then I may express who I would love to be as follows:

<u>Be</u>: I see myself as balanced, being the person I want to be in my life.

What do I see myself doing?

<u>Do</u>: I open my mind to possibility, knowing I can do whatever it takes or whatever I need to do to be the person I want to be.

What would I see myself having?

<u>Have</u>: I know I have the perceptiveness and mental acuity to recognize the symmetry, the duality in persons and events so I may maintain the balance I need to continue my personal growth.

Mental Models - Leadership in Action

Knowing your own values gives you freedom, better control of your life and helps you develop healthier relationships. Another form of Have, Do, Be[41] is based on Dr. William Glasser's Choice Theory® and helps you determine if you have the beliefs that can sustain you in getting what you want. The activity also brings into awareness the limiting beliefs whereby people often sabotage or block themselves from getting what they want.

1	2	3	4	5	6
What do I **WANT**? List ten (10) things.	If I had what I wanted, what would I **HAVE**?	If I had . . . what would I **DO**?	If I had . . . & I would be doing . . . what would I **BE**?	Am I the person I say I want to be?	How am I sabotaging what I want? What are the underlying beliefs?
1. 2. 3. 4. 5. 6. 7. 8. 9. 10.					

Pair and share

List any ten things that you want for yourself. Then, switch notebooks with a partner and take turns asking one another the questions in columns 2 through 5.

Hand notebook back to your partner so each person can complete column 6.

All team members now reflect to see which beliefs are limiting them in getting what they want. Discuss the ways this activity applies to leadership.

Mental Models - Leadership in Action

> The brain is poorly designed for formal instruction. In fact, it is not at all designed for efficiency or order. Rather, it develops best through selection and survival.[42]
>
> Brain-Based Learning
> Eric Jensen

Eric Jensen, a teacher first and foremost, gained prominence when he co-founded SuperCamp, the first brain-compatible learning program for teens, in 1981. He is committed to making a lasting difference on how the world learns. Brain-compatible learning offers ways that the brain learns best and is rooted in multiple disciplines: biology, genetics, psychology, chemistry and neuroscience to name a few. Critics state that all learning involves the brain; however, brain-based learning is concerned with the ways that the brain learns "naturally" and offers a way of thinking about learning. It is not a formula but rather a vast range of strategies that have proven helpful to learning.

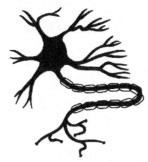

Eric Jensen offers seven steps in transforming schools into learning organizations.[43] They are offered here, with permission, to provide an opportunity for discussion and dialogue.

1.   Assess the Existing Culture

   - What is the existing culture in the organization?
   - How do you presently work within the culture?
   - What impact do you perceive yourself to have?

2.   Build a Collective Vision

   - What is your personal vision?
   - Does your personal vision align with the collective vision?
   - How do your personal and collective visions impact choices in your life?

Mental Models - Leadership in Action

3. Establish a Learning Climate
    - Describe the present environment in your organization.
    - How do you contribute to the present learning environment in your organization?
    - What changes are your prepared to make to effect change in the learning environment at work?

4. Encourage Personal Mastery
    - In what ways are you current about your job responsibilities?
    - What new learning and insights are you seeking?
    - How does the organization support personal mastery?

5. Promote Team Learning
    - What qualities do you perceive a team member to have?
    - In what ways do you see yourself as a team player?
    - Pair and share a story about how you collaborate in the workplace.

6. Systems Thinking is Everyone's Business
    - How would you describe "systems thinking?"
    - Cite some examples of how the system sometimes works against itself? What changes might you suggest within the system in your organization?

7. Nourish the Dream
    - What is the dream in your organization?
    - How often does the leadership engage teams in revisiting the dream?
    - What processes are in place to track progress and nourish the dream?

Mental Models - Leadership in Action

Jill and Steve Morris in their book *Leadership Simple, Leading People To Lead Themselves,* offer a process for individuals to change their behavior using a simple model[44] of human thought and action to improve individual and group performance within organizations. They offer ways to narrow "The Gap" between what people want and what they perceive they are getting. The model and process are based on Dr. Glasser's Choice Theory®, Reality Therapy and Lead Management. They identify three areas of leverage people can use to close the gap.

        People can:

1.   Change their perceptions
2.   Change what they want
3.   Change their behavior

Triangle of Choice

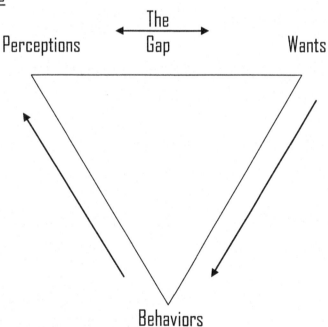

Using the scenario of an employee who doesn't like the new director of his department, share with a partner how you can effect change through the three areas of leverage outlined above.

Mental Models - Leadership in Action

. . . if I brought you down to the size of an individual cell so you could see your body from that perspective, it would offer a whole new view of the world. When you looked back at yourself from that perspective you would not see yourself as a single entity. You would see yourself as a bustling community of more than 50 trillion individual cells.[45]

The Biology of Belief
Bruce Lipton, Ph.D.

Bruce Lipton, a cell biologist by training, radically changed our understanding of life. His research shows that genes and DNA do not control our biology but that the DNA is controlled by signals from outside the cell, including the energetic messages emanating from our positive and negative thoughts. This breakthrough on the cell membrane presaged the new science of *Epigenetics.*

Some questions raised by Bruce Lipton.

1. Are you ready to use your conscious mind to create the life you want, flowing with health, happiness and love, without the aid of drugs?

2. Are you ready to consider a reality other than the medical model that views the human body as a biochemical machine?

3. Which beliefs do you hold that have you embracing archaic beliefs you have acquired from the scientific and media establishments?

4. Are you open to considering the exciting new possibilities offered by leading-edge science?

5. Share other advances you have read about.

Step 6 Embrace Diversity

> Members of the established corporate culture may find the qualities and characteristics of the new employees interesting and exciting. They may desire to spend time with the new employees but are reluctant to do so because of fear that they would be compromising their culture by cavorting with "outsiders." This hesitance to show acceptance of others can cause dissension within a company.[46]
>
> Leveraging Diversity at Work
> Kim Olver & Sylvester Baugh

"You should learn not to make personal remarks, Alice said with some severity: "It's very rude" [83]. Understanding the culture of an organization is one of the keys to effecting changes within it. I was amazed how challenging it was, as a new superintendent of a school district, to predict whether a motion would pass or not, after having had discussions with the Chair and other committee members. I quickly realized that I needed to read the culture more accurately through observation, attentive listening and dialogue. The job became one of the most rewarding of my career.

Kim Olver and Sylvester Baugh in *Leveraging Diversity at Work* speak of the dangers when leaders believe a target group needs special protection or special privileges. When leaders understand some of the concerns that different groups share and develop a strategic plan to embrace and celebrate those differences, maintaining a diverse and inspired workforce is more likely to occur.[47]

Dialogue

1. What labels do you bring to other cultures?
2. What are the underlying beliefs of those labels or biases?
3. Share a perception that you changed over time when you had more information.
4. How can you broaden your base of information about other cultures?

Embracing Diversity

Olver and Baugh offer standards for the majority and minority cultures so that leaders may become allies with the diverse groups within their organizations. Behaving with these standards in mind provides the organization with a benchmark to demonstrate its advocacy of diversity in the workplace. Below are some of the standards offered with permission.[48] The numbers refer to specific standards in *Leveraging Diversity at Work.*

1. Understand that racism, sexism, ageism, and other 'isms' are everywhere.
   - What type of 'ism' have you experienced in the workplace?
   - What differences are there between what is said and what is done by the leadership?

2. Learn about yourself and your heritage.
   - What can you share with others about your own heritage?
   - How are holidays or holydays from other cultures celebrated?

3. Leave your comfort zone.
   - What are the obstacles for you in leaving your comfort zone?
   - Share with a partner how you can risk leaving your comfort zone.

4. Give up denial.
   - How can you show you are ready for fair and equal treatment?
   - How can team members become a unified 'speaking voice?'

9. Take a public stand against injustice.
   - List some of the injustices in the workplace.
   - How would team members voice these injustices?

10. Maintain a clear and strong vision of the end result.
    - Revisit the visioning process within the organization.

Step 7 Trust Your Intuition

 We tend to rely on our more "advanced" and "civilized" senses, but remember that our most reliable senses are the ones that developed first [survival]. Our sense of touch develops before our sight, our intellect last of all. Nature tells us what we can count on to survive – and we were given intuition for a reason.[49]

Practical Intuition
Laura Day

"If anyone of them can explain it [the evidence], said Alice" who "had grown so large in the last few minutes that she even was a bit afraid of interrupting . . . I'll give him [the witness] sixpence" [148] which, of course, she didn't have. The court scene over the stolen tarts has Alice growing both literally and figuratively in confidence as she trusts her intuition about the sixpence.

Gavin De Becker, a personal security expert and consultant, explains how to use the power of intuition to identify and avoid danger in *The Gift of Fear*. Intuition is non-sequential, a 'knowing' without any use of conscious reasoning.[50] Whereas intuition and 'gut' feelings seem to be accepted since they relate to our survival, is there evidence that intuition plays a role in the decision-making process? Although it appears to be accepted that intuitive processes are critical for effective strategic decision-making, there is little in the way of applied research on the topic. There are, however, some interesting studies.

An article in the Journal of Managerial Psychology on "Intuition in Managers: Are intuitive managers more effective?" by Jon Aarum Andersen suggests that intuition as a decision-making style appears to be related to organizational effectiveness. Although several managers are intuitive, it remains to be seen whether intuitive managers are more effective than others. The study was based on two hundred managers from eight companies. If intuition is an indicator of creativity and innovation, then the study found that almost 25% of all managers were primarily intuitive when problem-solving and making decisions.

The Role of Intuition in Decision-Making

An investigation of thirty-three managers and their problem-solving and decision-making styles provided some insight. The 'creative-innovative' decision-making style was found in 23% of the managers.[51]

Herbert A. Simon in his article "Making Management Decision: the Role of Intuition and Emotion" states that some direct evidence suggests that the intuitive skills of managers depend on the same kinds of mechanisms as the intuitive skills of chess masters: a large amount of knowledge in memory; knowledge gained from training and experience; and knowledge organized in terms of recognizable chunks and associated information. Being an effective leader or manager means having command of a whole range of leadership/management skills and applying them as they become appropriate.[52]

We are conscious of only a small section of what we know. Intuition allows leaders to draw on that vast storehouse of unconscious knowledge that includes not only everything that one has experienced or learned either consciously or subliminally, but also the infinite reservoir of the collective or universal unconscious, in which individual separateness and ego boundaries transcend. Famous people in business such as Bill Gates, Steve Jobs, Oprah Winfrey, Jack Welch, Donald Trump and Sir Richard Branson have all pointed to intuition as a major factor in their decision-making processes.

Pair & Share

What criteria do you, as team members, bring to problem-solving?

Are they similar to what you bring to decision-making?

When have you listened to your intuition against reason?

What was the outcome of listening to your intuition?

What is your understanding of the role that intuition plays in decision-making?

Step 8 Teach the Language of Systems Thinking

Although systems thinking is seen by many as a powerful problem-solving tool, we believe it is more powerful as a language, augmenting and changing the ordinary ways we think and talk about complex issues.[53]

The Fifth Discipline Fieldbook
Peter Senge et al.

"– for it's all in some language I don't know,' utters Alice, over a poem in *Through the Looking-Glass"* [176]. The numerous books written about "Jabberwocky" suggest that many cultures have given it sense. Leaders, too, search for mirror-reflected meaning behind the looking glass in speaking a language that everyone in the organization understands. Senge states that farm children understand the cycles of cause and effect and know that at the time of a great flood, it is time to conserve water. These types of paradoxes are prevalent in organizational life. Here are some for your deliberation.

1. The company is enjoying its greatest growth period and the leadership believes it is time to plan for when business is slow.
2. The leadership tells everyone that the company resources are being drained but the workers perceive the recent policies are bringing in the greatest gains.

The organization requires what Senge calls 'peripheral' vision, paying attention to the world with a wide-angled lens. It is important to see the connection between your actions and how they interrelate to other areas of activity. It is more than just understanding the language; it is 'thinking' it, integrating it, until it becomes natural to you.[54]

In light of the above information, share within your team other paradoxes that you have discovered in your organization. How were these approaches successful?

Teaching the Language of Systems Thinking

Systems thinking, in its broadest sense, comprises methods, tools and principles that look at the interconnectedness of forces which are part of a common process. The one benefit of systems thinking language is in describing how to achieve meaningful change in organizations. This form of change was named 'system dynamics' by Professor Jay Forrester and his colleagues at Massachusetts Institute of Technology.[55]

Deliberate with team members on the following statements. Are they true or false? Explain how they relate to systems thinking?

1.   There are no right answers.

2.   You can redesign your system by dividing it into parts to see what is wrong in order to solve a problem.

3.   With systems thinking, it is imperative that team members collaborate with one another to find solutions.

4.   Sometimes it is best to do nothing.

5.   Once everyone has a good understanding and starts thinking 'systems,' you are well on your way and do not need to continually examine how the system is working.

6.   It is easier to find the fast solution by examining the system at the level of rules, physical structure and work processes.

7.   Systems thinking points out vulnerabilities and, as such, behavior gets worse before it gets better.

Teaching the Language of Systems Thinking

There are four levels operating simultaneously in an organizational setting.[56]

Level I	Events
Level II	Patterns of Behavior
Level III	Systems (Systemic Structure)
Level IV	Mental Models

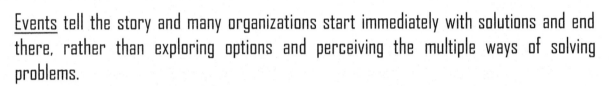

<u>Events</u> tell the story and many organizations start immediately with solutions and end there, rather than exploring options and perceiving the multiple ways of solving problems.

Team Approach

* What is your story about an event in your organization?
* How did you go about solving it?
* In what ways were your actions successful? Unsuccessful?
* What would you do differently had you the opportunity of viewing this issue again?

<u>Patterns of Behavior</u> refer to the behaviors of individuals and groups in the organization over a period of time. It is often necessary to retrace behaviors to three to four years before the event occurred in order to be able to see the pattern over time.

Team Approach

* What behaviors are leaders and team members engaged in presently?
* Trace the behavior back over at least a three-year period. What patterns do you see?
* What conclusions can be drawn from these patterns?
* Do you see a clearer path of action that is required?

Teaching the Language of Systems Thinking

<u>System Structure</u> encompasses the key interrelationship of factors within the organization.

Team Approach

* Brainstorm and list all the factors that you see at work in your organization?
* Relate how time variables in one or two factors created what appeared to be chaos?
* What course of action was taken?
* Was this course of action successful? Why or why not?

<u>Mental Models</u> are the assumptions held by people in the organization that are often unstated. They exist below the surface of awareness and shape how we act. Step 5 encourages us to be open to mental models so they may be examined, bringing them into our awareness so we can see perceive details we hadn't seen before.

<u>Arm Wrestling Activity</u>[57]

Configuration: People form pairs.

Objective: Arm wrestle with your partner, getting your partner's arm down as many times as possible.

Debrief: Share the behaviors you used to "win" as many times as possible.

Assumptions: What do you as team leaders believe about 'winning?' Did any pairs decide not to get as many 'wins' as possible? Why?

The above activity is an example of some people not being held back by the mental model that only one person can win. These are differences in perception since some people see details others don't see and these shapes their perceptions.

Step 9 Rethink Thinking

> . . . presencing is about 'pre-sensing' and bringing into presence – and into the present – your highest future potential. It's not just 'future' in some abstract sense but my own highest future possibility as a human being.[58]
>
> Presencing
> C. Otto Scharmer et al.

"Alice had begun to think that very few things were really impossible" [14]. Just as Peter Senge et al made the biggest breakthroughs in the 90's on how leaders and organizations viewed themselves, it is Peter Senge, C. Otto Scharmer, Joseph Jaworski and Betty Sue Flowers that offer *Presence* and the **U** theory which explores the elements of profound change in people, organizations and society. It is to see, sense and realize possibility in ourselves, organizations, institutions and society itself.

As we move down the left side of the **U**, we see and sense the world as something 'given.' We begin to shift perceptions from <u>sensing</u> to <u>seeing</u> from the "the living process underlying reality." As we move up the right side of the **U**, we start to experience the world as unfolding through us.[59]

Self – as observer of exterior world (creation of the past)

transforms into

Self – source through which the future begins to emerge
Shift or reversal from Observer to Source is called "Presencing."

What do you understand 'presencing' to mean? What are implications for you and for an organization?

Rethinking Thinking

The authors of *Presence* encourage readers to offer comments about their thinking about the book. Here is one reader's comment in his exact words:

 I spend a lot of time reading what could be called the more sophisticated end of general management literature and *Presence* is dramatically different in layout and approach. It is reflective and discursive, with a lot of forays into philosophical thinking and developments in scientific theory. Those who are used to a diet of "how to's," sidebars, summaries, and highlighted key points are likely to find it hard going. However, these are probably precisely the people who most need to absorb the ideas in the book. The argument of the book as a whole asserts that total reliance on dispassionate analytical rationalism is a sure path to the wrong answer and that we (individually and collectively) need to find ways to see the wholeness of life and to use our hearts and our intuition to become "part of a future that is seeking to unfold." While this worldview is still radical in business circles, it is not new, and in fact is part of a growing movement. The authors take a valuable further step both in explaining why a change is necessary and in sketching an approach to learning the profound transformations in perspective that are needed.

- Bill Godfrey, *Change Management Monitor Review Site, Australia*
  Presencing
  Reader Comments, [286].

Questions

1. What changes do you see if we are to create sustainable food systems?

2. Brainstorm questions that arise out of the above reader's comment.

3. What direction are you taking in answering some of these questions?

Rethinking Thinking

> We must pay respect to water, and feel love and gratitude, and receive vibrations with a positive attitude. Then, water changes, you change, and I change. Because both you and I are water.[60]
>
> The True Power of Water
> Masaru Emoto

The water that makes up such a large part of our physical body and the water of the earth can be healed and transformed through our intentions to be grateful and thankful and to grow in love as one with the universe. Masaru Emoto in *The Hidden Messages in Water* offered the world pictures of how our thoughts and words and music effect changes in the water crystals. In *The True Power of Water* Emoto speaks of HADO, the Healing And Discovering Ourselves. Hado is "all the subtle energy that exists in the universe."[61] Each thought carries its own Hado and is displayed in the crystals. Hado is energy so when two people, for example, have the same frequency and resonate, we call it 'friendship' or 'love.'

Situation: You don't like your boss because you and he think so differently.
              How Can You Change Your Thinking? [See total behavior, p. 66].

Situation: Your boss doesn't like the way you do things?
              What can you do about this? What can he do about this?

Dr. Emoto can measure vibrations and offers ways to cancel those vibrations that are destructive to us. Dr. William Glasser through Choice Theory® and Total Behavior offers specific ways we can change our acting and thinking in order to bring our feelings and physiology into alignment with mental health and happiness. The car is the perfect analogy to help us understand how we can take control of our lives. Although we do not choose our diseases, Dr. Glasser explains that "disease" occurs when we are out of balance to such an extreme degree, that the physiological component of the car becomes 'the car' and disease may ensue.

Rethinking Thinking – Dr. Glasser's Total Behavior

> All we can do from birth to death is behave. All behavior is total behavior and is made up of four inseparable components: acting, thinking, feeling, and physiology.[62]
>
> Choice Theory:
> A New Psychology of Personal Freedom
> William Glasser, M.D.

Dr. Glasser offers the car as an analogy for behavior and it is one which almost all people I have worked with over the years understand well from the smallest child to the 'preferred citizen.' Dr. Glasser explains that all behavior is purposeful and consists of four components: acting, thinking, feeling and physiology or what I often refer to as 'body talk,' all happening concurrently. We may give as an example "That man is debating right now." The debating or 'acting' component may be more apparent but accompanying the act of debating and integral to it is a thinking component, feeling component and also physiology. Dr. Glasser further explains that we have more direct control over our acting and thinking and less over our feeling and physiology. We must change our acting or thinking in order to effect changes in our feelings and physiology.

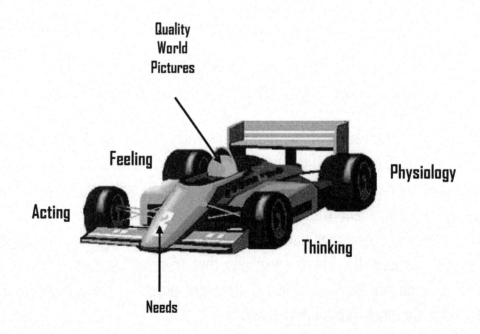

Rethinking Thinking - Dr. Glasser's Total Behavior

The car may also serve as a metaphor for Choice Theory® itself. The driver of the car is the Quality World picture we have in our head of what we want. We drive the car and choose the direction in order to meet the Quality World picture to satisfy one or more of the basic needs for love and belonging, power, freedom, fun and survival. The driver makes choices and is continually comparing what he perceives he is getting against what he wants. He sees how far or how close he is to his destination in meeting the picture he wants now. The car represents for many a new way of thinking about 'thinking.' Teaching and applying Choice Theory® within your organization may serve it well.

Which car are you driving?[63] Choose one of the cars below and share your story about the car with 'you' as the driver. Explain your behavior in terms of the four components of total behavior. E.g. I drove this car to work and got caught in a traffic jam that made me late for a new job interview. [now, describe your total behavior as you sit there, waiting. You have also forgotten your cell phone].

Rethinking Thinking

> Yet no matter how well or sick we may currently be, we still
> have the ability to choose our thoughts and feelings, and select
> those that support peak vitality. I call this the *epigenetic
> health cycle*.[64]
>
> The Genie in Your Genes
Dawson Church, Ph.D.

According to Dr. Church there is a wide variety of internal epigenetic interventions we can make to support peak health: positive beliefs, nurturing beliefs, visualizations, heart coherence, spirituality, meditation, attitude, prayer and altruism. We should avoid those behaviors that do not support optimum health. In this way, we reduce stress and promote life-enhancing hormones and beneficial substances in our bodies.[65]

 The following is a synopsis of a presentation, **Making the Quantum Leap: How much impact do our thoughts really have?** offered by Jean Seville Suffield and Lynn Sumida at The William Glasser Institute International Conference in Seattle, Washington, July 2007 on ideas taken from *The Biology of Belief* by Bruce Lipton, *The Genie in Your Genes* by Dawson Church and Sumida's work with her own company Miruspoint.®

This presentation explored how deeply impactful our thoughts really are. Given the current focus on "manifesting" as evidenced by DVDs like *The Secret*, it is relevant to look at how well we understand this kind of thinking. The well-known axiom of "Whether you think you can or can't, you are right!" suggests the power of thoughts. But today we can go much, much further.   We now have the science to look at things on a much deeper level, far beyond "positive thinking." Dr. Emoto's video, *The Hidden Messages in Water*, shows through the use of water crystals, the power of thought on physical matter. This information was first seen in the Hollywood movie, *What The Bleep Do We Know?* The information challenges the belief that matter is static and that we are not really influencing our environment.

Rethinking Thinking

It demonstrates vividly that what we 'think' does, in fact, affect what goes on around us. Dr. Bruce Lipton's latest video, *Nature, Nurture and the Power of Love* demonstrates at the cellular level, the power of thought and ultimately, consciousness. Both of these DVD's are worth viewing, if you want to challenge your beliefs about how we impact our world, internally and externally.

The Biology of Belief

Research shows that genes and DNA do not control our biology, that instead DNA is controlled by signals from outside the cell – including the energetic messages emanating from our positive and negative thoughts.

Epigenetics is the study of the signals that turn genes on and off [chemical and electromagnetic], inside and outside the body.

Genes are not static – genes turn on and off!

SIGNALS

Implications for Health

1. What interferes with the signals and impedes health? STRESS +

2. Share with a partner the stressors you experience in your life.

3. In what ways do we alter the baseline and raise our own stress levels?

4. What signals do you get from your body while under severe stress? Do you pay attention? Why or why not?

Rethinking Thinking

Some Revelations from *The Genie in Your Genes* by Dawson Church.

A) DNA is not Destiny
   Studies in mice show that we can change gene expression without making changes to the DNA. Bruce Lipton had raised the question of nature and nurture. What we now see from the work of Dawson Church and others is that consciousness trumps both nature and nurture.

   What are the implications for the way we live our lives?

B) Childhood Stress Results in Adult Disease
   There is a link between childhood stress and disease.

   How important is this knowledge for families and the ways in which the family members interrelate to one another?

C) You are the Director of the Gene Show
   There are certain lifestyle factors that affect health and longevity. Yet there is mounting evidence that invisible factors of consciousness and intention play an important role in the epigenetic control of genes

   What changes can you make as the Director?

D) Beliefs and Biochemistry
   Consciousness and intention and factors such as beliefs, feelings, prayers [the benevolent God versus the punishing God], and attitudes play leading roles in the epigenetic control of genes.

   What are your beliefs around this statement?

Rethinking Thinking

E) Psychology Becomes Physiology

Marked physiological changes were made within thirty days for one half of the group of eighty-four maids who cleaned hotel rooms, when they heard a brief presentation on how their work qualifies as good exercise. The other half did not. The results, albeit, on a small scale, were astounding.[66]
- loss of an average of 2 lb.
- lowered blood pressure by almost 10 per cent
- drops in body-fat percentage, body mass index, and waist- to-hip ratio

Is there a value you can bring to your work that you had not thought about before?

F) Prayer is Good Medicine [Questions are for reflection – Option to share]

There have been hundreds of studies whereby prayer leads to significant changes in health.

Do you turn to prayer? When and how does this help you?

If you do not belong to a formal religion, is there a higher purpose, essence, or life force in which you believe?

G) Doing Good Does You Good

Studies have shown that acts of altruism prolong lives.

Has your life changed in any way from acts of altruism?

How has being a volunteer improved your attitude toward life?

Rethinking Thinking

H) Seven Minutes of Spirituality
Spiritual nurturing affects healing. Studies have shown how a doctor's bedside manner affects the patient's quality of life.

Relate your story [optional] or that of a family member or friend of a time when the doctor made a difference by speaking often with you and/or visiting with you in hospital.

I) Meditation
Brain scans record areas of the brain being actively engaged during meditation with Tibetan monks.

The monks showed increase in gamma waves, the type involved in attention, memory and learning and linked to positive emotions like happiness.

School teachers trained in Buddhist techniques and, who meditated less than 30 minutes per week, improved their moods.

J) Epigenetic Visualization

The Simontons were pioneers in this field in the 70's. There are innumerable documented cases about the effect of visualization techniques on health and healing. Carol Sweck, Ph.D. a research psychologist at Stanford University noticed that students held beliefs about the nature of intelligence. Some believed intelligence was fixed and others believed that intelligence can grow and develop. She compared the math scores of the two groups over a two-year period. The students who believed that intelligence can grow had increased scores while the other group's scores had decreased. [67]

How has a change in some of your beliefs impacted your life?

Rethinking Thinking

K) Attitude is Everything

Negative perceptions about aging can shorten our life while positive beliefs prolong it. Dr. Andrew Weil in his book, *Spontaneous Remission*, cites several studies on attitude.

Recall a change in attitude that you made recently. A shift in others?

How has the change in attitude helped you? Others?

L) Why Stress Hurts

There is much research on stress and its effects on the body. The work of Robert Sapolsky, Eric Jensen, Dawson Church and so many others reveal the dangers of sustained stress. Stress affects:[68]

- DHEA associated with protective and health-promoting functions, and longevity
- repair and replacement of most kinds of cells
- wound healing
- levels of circulating immune cells and antibodies
- life of brain cells
- muscle mass
- bone loss
- generation of new skill cells
- fat accumulation around waist and hips, reduced memory and learning abilities.

What is your baseline for stress?

How do you raise this baseline which becomes the new norm?

Rethinking Thinking

What factors increase stress in this day and age of rapid change?

How are you handling some of them?

What is your plan for the future to reduce stressors in your life?

M) Engineering Your Cells Consciously

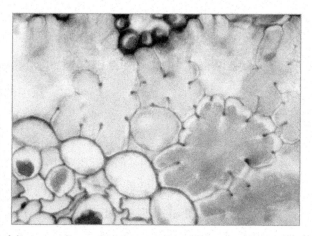

The increased cortisol levels associated with severe stress work on our bodies as outlined above. In fact, there are over 1,400 chemical reactions and over thirty hormones and neurotransmitters that shift in response to stressful stimuli. So, by de-stressing ourselves, we are then able to take a leading role in determining which instrument we wish to play in our genetic symphony. In self-healing with every thought, feeling and belief, we are performing epigenetic engineering on our own cells. Celebrate with great joy!

The Epigenetic Health Cycle may be found on page 72 of *The Genie in Your Genes.*

What are your Quality World pictures of health for yourself?

In what ways are you tipping the scales of your health?

What types of thinking are you going to shed?

What action plan can you consider to improve your health?

What type of commitment are you giving to the plan?

Step 10 Take Time

Alice spotted the White Rabbit hurrying down another long passage. "Oh my ears and whiskers, how late it's getting!" [12] cried the Rabbit. "I think you might do something better with the time," [Alice] said, "than wasting it in asking riddles that have no answers" [86]. Preoccupation with Time permeates the Alice books: Time turned upside, Time running backwards, distorted time, tardiness, and time mattering not at all. As a leader, take time for:

- ➤ reflection & affirmations
- ➤ relationships that matter
- ➤ mental health
- ➤ physical health
- ➤ intention

Reflection

1. Take time each day to reflect on your life's purpose.

2. How does your life purpose tie in with your beliefs?

3. What books are you presently reading to help you de-stress yourself?

4. List the areas of your life that you would like to change right now.

    Areas To Change

    ➤
    ➤

    What are you presently doing to effect change in each area?

    How do you know that the choices you are making are leading you in the direction you want to go?

Taking Time

Affirmations for Step 1

Be Clear

➢ I know that I can align my beliefs with the way I see living my life right now.

➢ I am loving and capable and know I make clear choices.

➢ I offer gratitude into the world to give me clarity of purpose.

➢ My choices are shaping how I want to live my personal life.

➢ The vision I see for my personal life is clear to me.

➢ I am certain about the clarity of my life's purpose.

Reflect on being clear about your life's purpose and write several affirmations of your own.

➢

➢

➢

➢

➢

➢

➢

➢

Taking Time

Affirmations for **Step 2**

Build a **S**hared **V**ision

➤ I know that I can align my beliefs with those of my work right now.

➤ I am loving and capable and make effective choices at work.

➤ I offer gratefulness into the world to give me clarity of purpose at work.

➤ My choices are shaping how I want to live my professional life.

➤ The vision I see for my professional life is clear to me.

➤ I am certain about my purpose within the organization for which I work.

Reflect on your shared vision and write several affirmations of your own.

➤

➤

➤

➤

➤

➤

➤

➤

➤

Taking Time

Affirmations for Step 3

Surrender Control

- ➢ I am capable of controlling only my own life.

- ➢ I surrender my control to the universe.

- ➢ I embrace the habits that help me surrender control over others.

- ➢ My choices are shaping how I am giving up controlling others.

- ➢ I can only control myself.

- ➢ I model that I can only control myself within the organization.

Reflect on surrendering control and write several affirmations of your own.

- ➢

- ➢

- ➢

- ➢

- ➢

- ➢

- ➢

- ➢

Taking Time

Affirmations for **Step 4**

Build **L**earning **N**etworks

➢ I am capable of collaborating with others within the workplace.

➢ I am loving and open my heart to those at work.

➢ I embrace the habits that help me build relationships with others at work.

➢ My choices help me in building the learning networks I need at work.

➢ I only control myself and model this with colleagues.

➢ I cooperate and collaborate in my dealing with others.

Reflect on networking and write several affirmations of your own.

➢

➢

➢

➢

➢

➢

➢

➢

➢

Taking Time

Affirmations for Step **5**

Be Open To Mental Models

➢   I am open to new ideas.

➢   I embrace other mental models to check for understanding.

➢   I offer mental models for scrutiny within my organization.

➢   My choices help me in being open to other mental models.

➢   I encourage others at work to share mental models with me.

➢   I cooperate and collaborate with my colleagues.

Reflect on being open to other mental models and write several affirmations of your own.

➢

➢

➢

➢

➢

➢

➢

➢

➢

Taking Time

Affirmations for **S**tep **6**

Embrace **D**iversity

➢ I am open to other cultures.

➢ I offer understanding and love of nations to the universe.

➢ I am loving to everyone in the workplace.

➢ My choices help me in opening up to diversity.

➢ I influence others at work by modeling inclusion.

➢ I cooperate and collaborate with all my colleagues.

Reflect on embracing diversity and write several affirmations of your own.

➢

➢

➢

➢

➢

➢

➢

➢

➢

Taking Time

Affirmations for **Step 7**

Trust Intuition

➢   I am open to what my inner voice tells me.

➢   I trust my intuition.

➢   I pay attention to my intuition with family and friends.

➢   I pay attention to my intuition regarding my work.

➢   I find a balance with intuition and skills in decision-making.

➢   I offer my acceptance of intuitive forces at work in the universe.

Reflect on trusting intuition and write several affirmations of your own.

➢

➢

➢

➢

➢

➢

➢

➢

➢

Taking Time

Affirmations for **Step 8**

Teach the Language of Systems Thinking

➢ I understand the wholeness of things.

➢ I know that the whole is more than the sum of its parts.

➢ I am open to different ways of thinking about systems.

➢ I understand that one change in a system impacts the whole system.

➢ I am influential in teaching systemic change within my organization.

➢ I am capable of demonstrating what systems are all about.

Reflect on teaching the language of systems thinking and write several affirmations of your own.

➢

➢

➢

➢

➢

➢

➢

➢

Taking Time

Affirmations for Step 9

Rethink Thinking

➢ I embrace thinking about 'thinking' in different ways.

➢ I offer my willingness to rethink 'thinking' to the universe.

➢ I am open to different ways of thinking.

➢ I know the universe sends me ways of challenging my present thinking.

➢ I influence others at work by rethinking 'thinking.'

➢ I am capable of handling all challenges that confront my way of thinking.

Reflect on rethinking thinking and write several affirmations of your own.

➢

➢

➢

➢

➢

➢

➢

➢

➢

Taking Time

Affirmations for **Step 10**

Take Time For Myself

➢ I take time for myself every day.

➢ I offer my time for myself as a blessing for mental health.

➢ I am open to different ways of taking time for myself.

➢ I take time for reflection at work.

➢ I influence others at work by taking some time for myself.

➢ I provide balance by taking time at home and at work.

Reflect on taking time and write several affirmations of your own.

➢

➢

➢

➢

➢

➢

➢

➢

➢

Taking Time

Affirmations for Step 10

Take Time For Relationships That Matter

➢ I love my family.

➢ I treasure the relationship I have with family members.

➢ I am open to seeing my family as they are.

➢ I accept that I can only change myself.

➢ I am open to changing my perceptions of others at work.

➢ I acknowledge and celebrate differences between myself and others.

Reflect on taking time for relationships that matter and write several affirmations of your own.

➢

➢

➢

➢

➢

➢

➢

➢

Taking Time

Affirmations for Step **10**

Take Time For Your Mental Health

➢   I am responsible for my own thoughts.

➢   I invite joy into my world every day.

➢   I am mentally able to lead my life to its fullest.

➢   I see how each experience I have enriches my life.

➢   I meditate each day and offer these thoughts to the universe.

➢   I rejoice in the successes of others.

Reflect on taking time to improve your mental health and write several affirmations of your own.

➢

➢

➢

➢

➢

➢

➢

➢

Taking Time for Your Physical Health

Affirmations for **Step 10**

Take Time For Your Physical Health

➢ I love my body.

➢ I exercise each day to keep my body healthy.

➢ I eat a balanced diet to support body health.

➢ I accept the body I have with all its wonders.

➢ I laugh often each day.

➢ I take care of my body.

Reflect on taking time to improve your physical health and write several affirmations of your own.

➢

➢

➢

➢

➢

➢

➢

➢

Taking Time for Your Intention

Affirmations for Step 10

Take Time For Your Intention

➢ I know I am the passageway of influencing others.

➢ I rejoice in my intention to live my life to its fullest.

➢ I live each day with love and appreciation for what I have.

➢ I know that I can make a difference in the world.

➢ I join the universe in offering joy and peace to others.

➢ I have a positive attitude toward myself and others.

Reflect on taking time to express your intention and write several affirmations of your own.

➢

➢

➢

➢

➢

➢

➢

➢

What's on the *Menu* The A-Mazing Maze[69]

The Maze represents how we behave in life. It holds up a mirror to help us evaluate if the behaviors we are choosing are helpful to us in reaching our goals. This activity applies extremely well to a business organization.

Maze Master: Jean Seville Suffield

Maze: A 6 x 9 foot square grid of 54 squares

Team: Group of 12 people

Objective: To discover the path according to the directions given by the Maze Master in order to help the team move safely through the Maze in the least amount of time possible

Maze Master: **1)** Predetermines the path through the Maze without revealing the path, **2)** Reviews the main points with participants, **3)** Demonstrates how the path may be discovered, and **4)** Says "Beep" when a participant steps on an incorrect square.

Instructions:
- Only one person at a time may attempt the Maze with forward, backward, and/or diagonal moves
- Both feet must remain in the square before the "beep" sounding an incorrect square or a "nod of the head" indicating a correct square given by Maze Master
- Participant backs out of the Maze at the sound of the "beep" and the next participant then begins to walk the Maze
- No languages are permitted although "sounds" are encouraged
- No props are permitted
- Teams will be timed and informed of time used
- A "return" beep adds a minute to the team's time
- Three to five minutes are given for planning strategies

Remember that this is a team activity. Enjoy!

What's on the Menu The Maze

The Debrief

Sharing Gems

What aspects of the activity worked well for you?

What specifically did you do to help one another?

Mirror Analogy

What behaviors did you choose that were in your best interest? The group's interest?

During the planning stage, what role did you play? Leader – Assistant – Director?

Did the role you chose help you to do what you wanted to do throughout the activity?

How do the behaviors chosen by the group mirror life?

How do the behaviors chosen by the group mirror your organization?

Karate Kid

Did you ever hesitate?

Did you consider this hesitation a mistake?

Describe your behavior at the sound of the first "beep."

The group's? Subsequent beeps? How do you handle mistakes in your organization?

What's on the *Menu* The Maze

Choice

If or when you stepped on a square that "beeped," what did you hear from the team?

Compare your total behavior [Acting-Thinking-Feeling-Physiology] before, during and after the activity.

How did your behaviors change throughout the activity?

Metaphor(s)

Where in your life are you standing, waiting to take a step, thinking: "No, what if I don't make it?" Describe an instance from your work.

Thinking of some choices you have made in your life, how would you describe yourself? [person of action . . .]

How would you describe yourself at work?

Doing What You Want to be Doing

You are the only "you" on your path, ready or not to put your foot down and say:

> This is what I want. This is what I plan
> to be doing to get what I want.

Are you doing what you want to be doing at work right now?

Are your values and beliefs aligned with those of your organization?

Share with the larger group the value of this activity for leadership.

What's on the *Menu* A System of Beliefs[70]

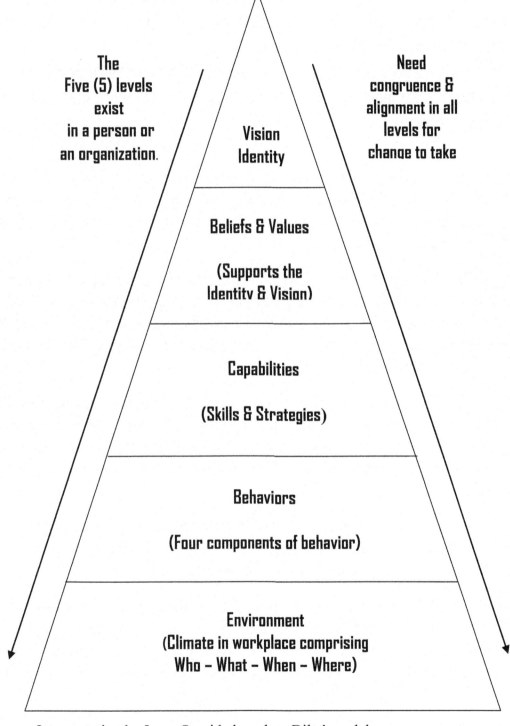

The
Five (5) levels
exist
in a person or
an organization.

Need
congruence &
alignment in all
levels for
change to take

**Vision
Identity**

Beliefs & Values

(Supports the
Identity & Vision)

Capabilities

(Skills & Strategies)

Behaviors

(Four components of behavior)

Environment
(Climate in workplace comprising
Who – What – When – Where)

Interpretation by Lynn Sumida based on Dilts' model.

What's on the *Menu* A System of Beliefs

Beliefs: Pathways to Health and Well-Being by Robert Dilts helps us discern how our beliefs fit into an overall system. He has identified five (5) logical levels that exist either in a person or in an organization. There must be congruence or alignment in the levels if one is to achieve harmony, health or productivity.

The farther down the level one goes, the more specific the factors being described. The higher up on the list, the more inclusive the factors are and the more the lower levels are affected by a change.

Identity: Change at this level is a change in identity and answers questions as "Who am I?" or "What is our mission?" Physiologically, this involves deep life-sustaining functions such as the immune system and endocrine system. An example would be "My mission in life is sharing who I am with others so that I may learn from them."

Values and Beliefs: Change at this level is a change in motivation and permission. It answers the question "Why do I do what I do?" and raises permission and motivation. Physiologically, this involves unconscious responses such as heart rate, pupil dilation, blood pressure, and the like. Examples: "Each of us is doing the best we know how to do." "The most important values in life include loving, being, fulfillment and enlightenment."

Capabilities: Change at this level is a change in direction and ability and answers the questions "How do I satisfy my values?" "Of what am I capable?" Physiologically, this includes semiconscious action such as eye movement, posture and the like. Examples: "I am capable of being honest with myself and there are times when this is more difficult." "When I realize that I have limited myself, I am able to introduce new choices."

Behaviors: Change at this level is remedial change and answers the question "What do I actually do?" Physiologically, this includes conscious actions under the control of the motor system. Examples: "I feel comfortable when talking with friends." "I eat healthy food sometimes."

Environment: Change at this level is remedial, involving changing location or altering some aspect of the situation. It answers the question "Where, when, and in what external context do I live?" Physiologically, this includes sensations and reflex actions, involving peripheral nervous system. Examples: "The stock market situation is putting many of us under stress." "Vitamins keep me healthy."

[From Lynn Sumida with permission.][71]

What's on the *Menu* Communication in Organization

How Do You Communicate Within Your Organization?

This section is an option if you understand choice theory and can facilitate reality therapy in working through conflict situations in the workplace.

1. Worker who feels unfairly passed over for a promotion – speaking with supervisor.

2. A 50 year old man who has just lost his job and has only worked in one place with one job skill – speaking with a company counsellor.

3. A 45 year old woman who feels stuck in her secretarial job and wants to move but has been there ten years – talking to her immediate superior.

4. You are an office supervisor and need to speak with a worker who consistently insists on 'doing his own thing' instead of the assigned work.

5. You are a personnel supervisor and have to speak with a worker who calls in sick quite often and mainly on Mondays.

6. You are a young kid on the line at work who is learning the job, but making tons of mistakes – talking to the line supervisor and mentor who has called him in.

7. Assembly line worker who feels like her supervisor is treating her unfairly – talking to a colleague.

8. Choose your own scenario.

HipBone Game

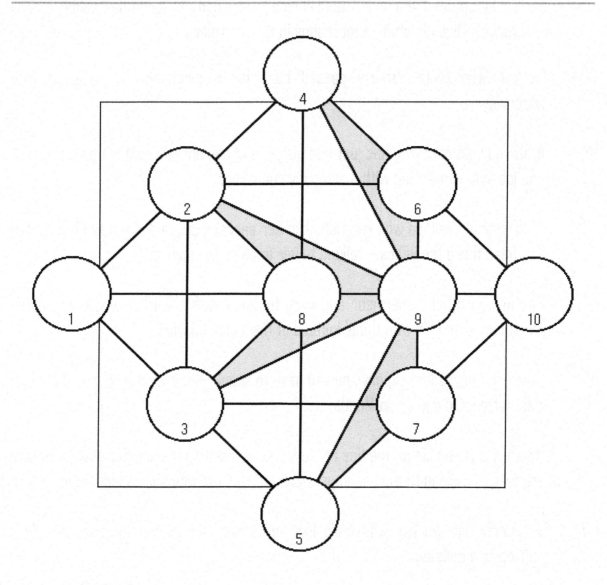

[Game and original Board by Charles Cameron, printed with permission.
See endnote for entry.]

There are many ways to play the HipBone Game. Have fun with the ones that follow!

HipBone

The object of the game is to demonstrate how your story is related   to the other ones already presented.   In teams of five and in a predetermined   order:

- ➢ Choose one of the words in the list below.
- ➢ Place your word inside one of the circles.
- ➢ Create a story for each one of the words that is related to all the other words [circles] that directly touches the word you have just added.
- ➢ Be imaginative and have fun.

Here is the list of words:

decision-making	collaboration
leadership	sales
quality	temperature
corporate structure	production quotas
creativity	office equipment

Game # 2

- ➢ Choose one of the steps to dynamic leadership outlined in this book.
- ➢ Place your word [step] inside one of the circles.
- ➢ Create a story for each one of the words [steps] that is related to all the other words [steps] that directly touches the word you have just added.
- ➢ Enjoy!

HipBone

<u>Game # 3</u> [This one is based on a knowledge of *Alice's Adventures in Wonderland* &
Through the Looking-Glass].

> ➢ Match what you perceive to be the best description of any one of the metaphors
>   from the two Alice Books to the Steps to Dynamic Leadership.
> ➢ Place your metaphor inside one of the circles.
> ➢ Create a story for each one of the metaphors that is related to the Steps and
>   directly touches the word you have just added.
> ➢ Be imaginative and have fun!

<u>Metaphors</u>   Cheshire Cat   Rabbit Hole

     Game of Chess   Mouse (Muse)

     Alice   White Rabbit

     Looking Glass   Jabberwock

     Mad Hatter [Adder] Pawn

<u>Ten Steps</u>   Rethink Thinking   Take Time   Intuition

     Shared Visioning   Learning Networks   Diversity

     Surrendering Control Clarity   Embrace Mental Models

     Teach the Language of Systems   Thinking

<u>Game # 4</u>

In teams of five, brainstorm and develop your own game using the WaterBird Board –
HipBone concept created by Charles Cameron, similar to the ones above or "Go for it!"
and develop one altogether different.

HipBone

Each team member takes a turn [twice in a team of 5 people] in answering any one of the questions below. Write the answer in order starting with number 1.

Once the ten [10] questions have been answered, the team determines the interconnectedness of the answers and arrives at a central theme.

What do we call . . .

1. providing preliminary discourse serving as an introduction?

2. asking or drawing one in?

3. engaging one or more people in everyday or specific topics?

4. considering options?

5. conversing and shaking apart various issues or topics?

6. placing in an inoperative state?

7. taking a side in discussing the pros and cons of an issue?

8. conversing on various issues in a logical and analytical manner?

9. engaging in discussion with no restrictions but high energy?

10. exploring the non-physical, the ideas, the communication itself?

[Answers to Game #5 may be found on page 109 as endnote 73].

Alice's Ad-ventures – Where to Go from Here

Alice's Adventures in Wonderland and *Through the Looking-Glass and What Alice Found There* provide the framework for this book. The images, symbols and metaphors in the  Alice Books provide the significance of the growth and discovery in the development of a human being. These same metaphors may serve as the journey that leaders take when they embark upon the growth and development of their organizations.

In conclusion, *10 Steps to Dynamic Leadership* offers you ten paths essential to your journey into leadership. You know there are countless more that you may choose by extending your map and generating ideas that have limitless possibility.

If you believe that you can create your reality, that you can join with others in collective thought processes and tap into that vast quantum field of energy, then you can, indeed, change yourself, your organization and the world!

Works Cited

Allen, Richard, Ph.D. (2002). *Impact teaching: Ideas and strategies for teachers to maximize student learning.* Boston, MA: Allyn & Bacon.

Allen, Richard, Ph.D. (2001). *Train smart.* San Diego, CA: The Brain Store.

Arntz, William and Betsy Chasse. (2004) *What the Bleep Do We Know!?* (2006) DVD.

Byrne, Rhonda et al. (2006). *The Secret.* (Original Edition). DVD.

Caine, Geoffrey and Renate Caine. Eds. (1994). *Making Connections: Teaching and the Human Brain.* Menlo Park, CA: Addison-Wesley.

Carroll, Lewis, 1832 – 1898. *Alice's Adventures in Wonderland. More Annotated Alice: Alice's Adventures in Wonderland & Through the Looking-Glass: Illustrated by Peter Newell: with notes by Martin Gardner.* (1990). New York: Random House, Inc.

Church, Dawson, Ph.D. (2007). *The Genie in Your Genes: Epigenetic Medicine and the New Biology of Intention.* Santa Rosa, CA: Elite Books.

Day, Laura. (1996). *Practical Intuition: How to Harness the Power of Your Instinct and Make It Work for You.* New York: Random House, Inc.

De Becker, Gavin. (2004). *The Gift of Fear: Survival Signals That Protect Us.* New York: Bantam Paperback Books.

Demartini, John F. (2002). *The breakthrough experience.* California: Hay House Inc.

Emoto, Masaru. (2005). *The True Power of Water: Healing and Discovering Ourselves.* Hillsboro, Oregon: Beyond Words Publishing.

Emoto, Masaru. (2005). *The Hidden Messages in Water: Healing and Discovering Ourselves.* Hillsboro, Oregon: Beyond Words Publishing.

Works Cited

Glasser, William, M.D. (1998). *Choice Theory: A new psychology of personal freedom*. New York: HarperCollins Publishers.

Glasser, William, M.D. (2000). *Counseling with Choice Theory: The new reality therapy*. New York: HarperCollins Publishers.

Glasser, William, M.D. (2005). *Defining mental health as a public health problem*. Chatsworth, CA: The William Glasser Institute.

Hatswell, Judy. (2004). *Building quality relationships: Interviewing for success* [CD]. New South Wales, Australia: Judy Hatswell. Available at judyhats@bigpond.net.au

Honey, Ivan and Russell Deal. Illustrator and designer: Mat Jones. (2006), *Cars 'R' Us Kit*. St. Luke's Innovative Resources. Bendigo, Victoria (Australia).

Jensen, Eric. (2000). *Brain-Based Learning. The New Science of Teaching & Training*. Revised Edition. San Diego CA: The Brain Store.

Lipton, Bruce, Ph.D. (2005). *The Biology of Belief: unleashing the power of consciousness, matter, & miracles*. Santa Rosa, CA: Elite Books.

Lipton, Bruce, Ph.D. (2003). *Nature, Nurture and Power of Love*. DVD.

McFadden, Judy. (1988). How to Raise a Good Kid. Australia.

McTaggart, Lynne. (2008) *The Intention Experiment: Using Your Thoughts to Change Your Life and the World*. New Afterword by the Author. New York: Free Press.

Morris, Steve., & Morris, Jill. (2003). *Leadership simple: Leading people to lead themselves*. Santa Barbara, CA: Imporex International Inc.

Olver, Kim & Sylvester Baugh. (2006). *Leveraging Diversity at Work: How to Hire, Retain and Inspire a Diverse Workforce for Peak Performance and Profit*. Chicago, Illinois: Inside Out Press.

Works Cited

Peterson, Arlin V. Ed.D. Professor Emeritus, Texas Tech University. "Pete's Pathogram" published as A. Peterson & G. Parr. *Pathogram: A Visual Aid to Obtain Focus and Commitment* (Journal of Reality Therapy, Fall, 1982: 18-22)

Pierce, Kenneth L. (2007). *Using Lead Management on Purpose: Creating Excellent Products and Services for a Global Economy.* Lincoln, NE: iUniverse.

Sapolsky, Robert M. (1999). *Why zebras don't get ulcers: an updated guide to stress, stress-related diseases, and coping.* New York: W. H. Freeman and Company.

Senge, Peter et al. (2005). *Presence: An exploration of profound change in people, organizations, and society.* New York: Currency Doubleday.

Senge, Peter et al. (1994). *The fifth discipline fieldbook:* Strategies for building a learning organization. New York: Currency Doubleday.

Smith, Donn, & Sumida, Lynn. (2003). The extraordinary within: Welcoming change and unlocking our true essence. Canada: Friesens.

Wubbolding, Robert. (2001). *Reality yherapy for the 2f^{t} century.* Philadelphia, PA: Brunner-Routledge.

Wubbolding R., & Brickell, J. (2001). *A Set of Directions for Putting and Keeping Yourself Together.* Minneapolis MN: Educational Media Corporation.

Wubbolding R., & Brickell, J. (1999). *Counselling with Reality Therapy.* Bicester, Oxon, England: Speechmark Publishing, Ltd.

Wubbolding, Robert. (1996). *Employee motivation.* Knoxville, Tennessee: SPC Press, Inc.

New Resources

Choice Theory in Motion: An animation by Alexander Gittinger based on Dr. William Glasser's Choice
     Theory and "How the Brain Works." DVD (2010): A Caflama Films Production. Choice
     Theory® is a registered trademark of William Glassr, M.D. All Rights Reserved.

Glasser, William, M.D. (2011). *Take Charge of Your Life: How to Get What You Need with Choice
     Theory® Psychology.* Bloomington, IN: www.iuniverse.com. Glasser, William, M.D. (1998).
     Choice Theory: A new psychology of personal freedom. New York: HarperCollins Publishers.

Robey, Patricia A., Robert E. Wubbolding, & Jon Carlson, Eds. (2012). *Contemporary Issues in Couples
     Counseling: A Choice Theory and Reality Therapy Approach.* New York, NY: Routledge.

Wubbolding, Robert E., Ed.D. (2010) *Reality Therapy: Theories of Psychotherapy Series.* Washington,
     DC: APA Books.

Endnotes

[1] Designed by Charles Cameron, 1995. WaterBird Board - HipBone printed with permission. Charles Cameron may be contacted at hipbone@earthlink.net

[2] Gardner, "More Annotated Alice." 162.

[3] Game and original Board by Charles Cameron printed with permission. See first entry.

[4] Senge et al. "The Fifth Discipline Fieldbook," 204.

[5] The Fieldbook, 204. Adapted by Richard Coutu and Jean Seville Suffield for *Shared Visioning* Workshops.

[6] The Fieldbook, 204.

[7] The Fieldbook, 302. Definitions.

[8] The Fieldbook, 20.

[9] The Fieldbook, 204. Adapted by Richard Coutu and Jean Seville Suffield for *Shared Visioning* Workshops.

[10] The Fieldbook, 204. Adapted from personal visioning.

[11] The Fieldbook, 301.

[12] The Fieldbook, 204. Adapted from personal visioning.

[13] Inspired by model of online ethics course. Natural Therapies Certification Board. Similar activity found in "The Fifth Discipline Fieldbook," 210.

[14] Model of online ethics course. See previous entry.

[15] Jensen, Certification Training, "Teaching with the Brain in Mind," Adapted by J. Suffield.

[16] The Fieldbook, 38.

Endnotes

[17] Quotation by Martin Luther King, Jr., taken from the University of Pennsylvania - African Studies Center: "Letter from a Birmingham Jail" April 16, 1963.

[18] Glasser, "Choice Theory: A New Psychology of Personal Freedom," From Choice Theory® which forms the basis of all that Dr. Glasser teaches.

[19] Choice Theory: A New Psychology of Personal Freedom.

[20] Senge et al. "Presence," 103.

[21] The triangle, as a symbol to plot the needs, the quality world and for using reality therapy, has been used by many instructors within The William Glasser Institute: Richard Coutu, Diane Gossen, Jean Suffield and others. Jill and Steve Morris use the triangle as The Triangle of Choice in their book, "Leadership Simple."

[22] Pierce. "Using Lead Management on Purpose," 24.

[23] Originally demonstrated by William Powers in a seminar at Northeastern University, Massachusetts (1999), organized by Larry Litwack.

[24] Arlin V. Peterson, Ed.D. Professor Emeritus, Texas Tech University. "Pete's Pathogram" published as A. Peterson & G. Parr. *Pathogram: A Visual Aid to Obtain Focus and Commitment* (Journal of Reality Therapy, Fall, 1982: 18-22). Printed with persmission.

[25] The Fieldbook, 301.

[26] Glasser, "Defining Mental Health as a Public Health Issue," 2.

[27] Pierce, 71.

[28] Pierce, 84. Chapter 8.

[29] Sapolsky, "Why Zebras Don't Get Ulcers," 215.

[30] McFadden, "A Simple Way to Raise a Good Kid." Adapted with permission.

Endnotes

[31] McFadden, "A Simple Way to Raise a Good Kid." Adapted with permission.

[32] The Fieldbook, 216.

[33] Glasser, "How the Brain Works," Choice Theory® Chart, created by William Glasser, M.D. Printing 2008.

[34] Based on Dr. William Glasser's Choice Theory® and Reality Therapy. Activity developed by Jean Seville Suffield and Richard Coutu.

[35] Wubbolding, "Reality Therapy for the 21st Century."

[36] Sumida, Prime Potential™ explanation pp. 46 - 47. See entry in Works Cited for first book with Donn Smith. Lynn Sumida, co-founder and owner of Miruspoint Facilitators Inc., offers Prime Potential™ training. You may reach her at lynnsumida@miruspoint.com

[37] Sumida, Prime Potential™ Life Satisfaction Index, printed with permission.

[38] Caine & Caine, "Making Connections," 34.

[39] Demartini, "The Breakthrough Experience," Principle 33. Kenneth L. Pierce is a facilitator of *The Demartini Method*® offered through weekend workshops entitled "The Breakthrough Experience." You may reach him at ken@clarendonconsulting.com

[40] Pierce, "The Breakthrough Experience." From Jean Seville Suffield's personal notes from session in Charlottetown, PEI Canada, April 26 – 27, 2008.

[41] Originally developed by Barnes Boffey and widely used within The William Glasser Institute.

[42] Jensen, "Brain-Based Learning," 3.

[43] Brain-Based Learning, 363. With permission.

[44] Morris and Morris, "Leadership Simple," 15. Triangle of Choice, slightly modified from original. Printed with permission.

Endnotes

[45] Lipton, "Biology of Belief," 36.

[46] Olver and Baugh, "Leveraging Diversity at Work," 116.

[47] Leveraging Diversity at Work, 167.

[48] Leveraging Diversity at Work, 187. "Standards" headings printed with permission.

[49] Day, "Practical Intuition," 174.

[50] Practical Intuition, 175.

[51] Human Relations, Vol 53, No. 1, 57-86 (2000) *The role of intuition in strategic decision-making.*

[52] Herbert A. Simon, "Making Management Decisions: The Role of Intuition and Emotion," *Academy of Management Executive* 1, 1 (February 1987): 57-64.

[53] The Fieldbook, 88.

[54] The Fieldbook, 89.

[55] The Fieldbook, 89.

[56] The Fieldbook, 97.

[57] The Fieldbook, 110.

[58] Presence, 220.

[59] Presence, 236,

[60] Emoto, "The True Power of Water," 145.

[61] The True Power of Water, 145.

[62] Choice Theory: A New Psychology of Personal Freedom, Axiom 8.

Endnotes

[63] Honey, Ivan and Russell Deal. You may purchase "Cars 'R' Us" kits through www.innovativeresources.org

[64] Church, "The Genie in Your Genes," 73.

[65] The Genie in Your Genes, 73.

[66] The Genie in Your Genes, 63.

[67] The Genie in Your Genes, 67.

[68] The Genie in Your Genes, 71.

[69] Adapted from Dr. Rich Allen, Impact Learning, Inc.

[70] Adapted by Lynn Sumida from Robert Dilts, "Beliefs: Pathways to Health and Well-Being."

[71] Synopsis of the five levels by Lynn Sumida from "Beliefs: Pathways to Health and Well-Being."

[72] Designed by Charles Cameron, 1995. WaterBird Board - HipBone printed with permission.

[73] Adapted from Senge, 361. Answers to Game #5

1. prologue 2. invitation 3. conversation 4. deliberation 5. discussion 6. suspension 7. debate 8. skillful discussion 9. dialogue 10. metalogue

Overall theme: Evolution of Dialogue or Forms of Communication or Methods of Inquiry.

. . . *The Intention Experiment* reveals that the universe is connected by a vast quantum energy field. Thought generates its own palpable energy, which you can use to improve your life and, when harnessed together with an interconnected group, to change the world.

The Intention Experiment
Lynne McTaggart

Other Works by Jean Seville Suffield

With Richard Coutu. *The philosophers' circle: Visionary Leadership.*
Revised Edition. (1996)

Conflict resolution: Activities for classroom use – Creating a learning environment.
Revised Edition. (2003)

Action . . . take 1: Self-evaluation and the student-led conference.
Revised Edition. (2003)

20/20 + Leadership: Alternate models for enhancing self-evaluation and assessment! (2010)

A Role-Play Notebook: Questions that really make a difference.
Third Edition. (2012)

CPSIA information can be obtained
at www.ICGtesting.com
Printed in the USA
BVOW04s1107221117

501091BV00018B/1441/P

9 781105 621154